12 WAYS TO *Experience More* WITH YOUR HUSBAND

Cindi McMenamin

Italicized text in Scripture quotations indicate author's emphasis.

Cover by Dugan Design Group

12 WAYS TO EXPERIENCE MORE WITH YOUR HUSBAND

Published by Harvest House Publishers
Eugene, Oregon 97408
www.harvesthousepublishers.com

ISBN 978-0-7369-6867-6 (pbk.)
ISBN 978-0-7369-6868-3 (eBook)

Library of Congress Cataloging-in-Publication Data

Names: McMenamin, Cindi, 1965- author.
Title: 12 ways to experience more with your husband : more trust, more passion, more communication / Cindi McMenamin.
Other titles: Twelve ways to experience more with your husband
Description: Eugene, Oregon : Harvest House Publishers, 2018. | Includes bibliographical references.
Identifiers: LCCN 2017039039 (print) | LCCN 2017048706 (ebook) | ISBN 9780736968683 (ebook) | ISBN 9780736968676 (pbk.)
Subjects: LCSH: Marriage—Religious aspects—Christianity. | Husbands—Psychology.
Classification: LCC BV835 (ebook) | LCC BV835 .M346 2018 (print) | DDC 248.8/44—dc23
LC record available at https://lccn.loc.gov/2017039039

Printed in the United States of America

17 18 19 20 21 22 23 24 25 26 / BP-SK / 10 9 8 7 6 5 4 3 2 1

Contents

Where Is the Love?

I'll never forget the day I was cleaning out my top dresser drawer and found a treasure.

I almost threw out the stack of aged, yellowed papers, weathered by time and slightly torn on the edges. When I unfolded the papers and read through them, I instantly realized why I'd kept them all those years. On them were written words any woman would want to read over and over again, terms of endearment spilling out from a man's heart onto paper for his beloved.

> *Cindi,*
>
> *I have never met another woman like you. You are my fantasy, you are my dream. I love you beyond expression. How can I express my devotion to you? I can give you all of myself all of my days and hope that you see how much you mean to me. If you were to leave this place, my life would be pointless. You complete me like no other. I love you desperately.*
>
> *Your forever man,*
> *Hugh*

As I read those words, my eyes teared up. And then my heart dropped. *I haven't had a letter like this from him in years. Why doesn't he write like this to me anymore?*

I read through the rest of the worn love letters I had kept, dating back to the first few years that we were married, more than 25 years ago! All described the captivating woman he saw me as—the intriguing, irresistible woman I had hoped in my heart of hearts that I still was in his eyes.

Given all we've been through, given the unattractive sides of me that he has seen through the years, would he still describe himself as desperately in love with me?

And then a more pointed question: *Am I even the same woman I was when he wrote those letters?*

How I would love to believe that I haven't changed a bit through the years. That I am still the little lovely thing he fell in love with. And that *he* is the one who has changed and no longer appreciates me the way he once did. How easy it would be to continue to believe that he had become distant, more critical, less interested, and less passionate than he was the day we married. It was a little tougher to put that magnifying glass up to myself and ask if I was the one who let resentments build up or baggage get in the way.

Granted, marriage over time becomes messy. After you and your husband share the best of times and the worst of times, settle into a routine, let your guards down, and let each other see the worst in yourselves, it can be difficult to recover lost ground, get it all back, and experience with each other what you once did. But I wanted to receive those kinds of letters again. I wanted my husband to see me, once again, as the captivating woman he married. I wanted to feel like a young, cherished bride again. I wanted to experience *more* with my husband than what I had settled into the past several years.

I wanted to once again *be* the woman to whom my husband penned those letters.

We all change through the years, and hopefully for the better. I'd like to believe I am wiser today and far more mature than I was in my younger years. But I can tell you right now, I can also tend to be less spontaneous, less optimistic, more irritable, more disinterested, and more wounded relationally, which unintentionally causes me to respond to my husband differently than I used to.

There's an old axiom: Familiarity breeds contempt. It is human nature to take advantage of what we have. To let the novelty wear off. To grow bored with something. As time passes, the excitement and allure of marriage can gradually fade. We can so easily slip into routines or even resentments that keep us from being the women we once were and that keep us from treating our husbands as we once did. As a result, we find ourselves thinking, *I wish I could experience more with him. More trust. More passion. More communication. More understanding. More laughter.*

It is human nature to take advantage of what we have.

Just the other day a friend of mine vented her feelings to me: "Sometimes I wish my husband would see the best about me, but unfortunately, through the years he's seen the ugly too. How do you get over the baggage that builds up through the years and make your husband see you as you really are...not as the woman who has made mistakes and blown it through the years?" She was speaking my dilemma. I had asked that same question in my heart of hearts many times.

I realized if I was to be the cherished wife who receives another letter like the ones I found in my top dresser drawer, I would have to *become* that woman my husband wrote to so many years ago.

But What About...?

I imagine by now you're thinking, *But, Cindi, so much has changed.* Or maybe you're thinking:

The novelty of the relationship has worn off.

I've seen his bad moments...and he's seen mine.

I don't feel attractive around him anymore. In fact, I feel that he barely even notices me.

Or worse, you might be thinking, *Too much has happened for it to ever be the same again.*

Those thoughts you may be having have not only been mine at one time, but they've belonged to hundreds of other wives I've heard from over the past 18 years who have written to me or talked with me about their frustrations and complaints.

There were nights I would lie awake next to my husband, who was sleeping in sweet oblivion, and wonder how to turn back the clock and make him see me the way he once did—as the captivating woman he fell in love with. And so many times I wished I could have back that man I married...have him treat me the same way he used to. And then I realized there was only one way to recapture his heart: Be the woman I was and do the things I did when he first fell in love with me.

The apostle John recorded a vision of Christ saying to a first-century church, "You have forsaken the love you had at first. Consider how far you have fallen! Repent and do the things you did at first" (Revelation 2:4-5).

While that can be applied to our tendency to grow complacent in our relationship with God, it can be applied to our marriages as well. God is not the only One who recognizes when our enthusiasm for Him has waned. Our husbands recognize when our enthusiasm for them has waned too. They once received our admiration, our smiles from across the room, our focused attention, our constant giggles, our full vigor. Then life happened. Kids came. Work called. We gained a few pounds and a million distractions. And before we knew it...complacency set in.

God is not the only One who recognizes when our enthusiasm for Him has waned. Our husbands recognize when our enthusiasm for them has waned too.

This book you are holding in your hands is not a book about how to change your husband and make him treat you the way you want him to, or at least the way he once did. It's about how to *be* and *remain* the woman he fell in love with. It's about how to continue to be the love of his life. It's about how to never let your love and commitment toward him fade away. And it's about how to make your—and his—"forever" stick so that you *both* can experience more. More trust. More passion. More communication. More understanding. More forgiveness. And more of what you didn't realize your marriage was capable of.

Removing the Baggage

Before we start this journey, I want you to know where I'm coming from. Not only have I been where you are and seen my husband's heart come back around, but I continue to receive letters and e-mails from women like you nearly *every day* wondering what they can do to remove the baggage, rebuild love, and recapture their husband's heart.

I also hear the stories of transformed hearts and renewed relationships when wives are willing to grab hold of the principles I'm laying out in this book—the same principles I had to practice myself in order to experience more with my husband.

The most common mistakes that you and I tend to make in our relationships can be redeemed through practicing simple strategies in the heat of the moment that can draw your husband's heart back toward you and allow you to experience the excitement of your relationship once again. Most of the time it's a matter of recognizing some of the mistakes all wives tend to make that slowly dampen the relationship and smolder the flame.

Once we recognize the actions that deteriorate trust and strain a marriage, we can then reverse them by rebuilding the trust, passion, and love that once existed. That is made possible as we rely on the only One who can redeem, restore, and renew relationships.

We can reverse our mistakes by rebuilding the trust, passion, and love that once existed.

I believe one of the reasons wives are so unhappy in their marriages today is that we have expectations that are very different from our husbands. While we both want the same things (respect, love, companionship, security, intimacy), we go about trying to achieve them differently. In general, men are simple—and straightforward—in their expectations. We women, however, can be very complicated when it comes to expressing what we want and how we try to achieve it.

I want to share with you the ways you can, among other things, think it through, let it go, switch it up, light him up, close the gap, help him out, stick it out, and bring it back. And if you are willing to try each chapter's "Focus for the Week" and make the same changes I did, I promise you will have a chance to remove (or prevent) the relational baggage, recapture (or maintain) the heart of your husband, and rebuild (or grow) your marriage into one that is not only enduring but exciting once again.

I've done it in my own marriage. You can too.

Where Sparks Once Flew

In talking to men or women who are in the throes of a nasty divorce I often hear the words, "He never really loved me" or "She never once loved me" or "We never really loved each other."

I've never once bought that line.

Sure, circumstances over the years (and fresh wounds especially) can make a couple forget how they once felt for each other. But even in rocky seasons of a marriage, we must all admit that there was a spark—or many—at one time. There was a desperation on the part of you and your husband to be with each other. What once caused a fire of passion and determination within him to do what it takes to be with you is still simmering somewhere underneath the surface of that man. It's still there, even though there may very well have been struggles, frustration, pain, and piled-up wounds from doing life together. That spark in your husband's heart just needs to be unearthed, rekindled, and fanned into a flame to burn freely once again.

Yes, you can get back that twinkle in his eyes, that swagger in his step, that loving tone in his voice. Well, technically *you* can't. But there is One who can help you do what you commit to Him to do for the sake of honoring Him in your marriage. As you recognize some behaviors that need to be reversed, you can rely on God's help to start rebuilding, renewing, and regluing your relationship with your husband. And recapturing his heart can be the result.

As you recognize some behaviors that need to be reversed, you can rely on God's help to start rebuilding, renewing, and regluing your relationship.

The first step is to recognize some of the common relationship mistakes we wives tend to make. I've designed a quiz to help you identify your attitudes, behaviors, and perspectives that are most likely causing tension in the relationship or making him remain distant. (Yes, your husband has his own set of faults and weaknesses, but this book is addressing you and what *you* can do to bring back the love and experience more.) Although you can't control or change your husband, you can take responsibility for your own actions as much as it depends on you and begin to reap the positive results of a renewed way of approaching him. So, here goes.

Self-Assessment: Identifying the Baggage

I've put together a list of questions that deal with the most common struggles in marriage. Answer "yes" to the statements you believe best describe yourself when it comes to your relationship with your husband and "no" to the ones that don't apply. Try to answer as honestly as possible with what you *actually do*, not what you know you *should* do. The more truthful you are, the quicker you will be able to pinpoint areas of tension in the relationship:

I expect my husband to meet most, if not all, of my emotional needs.	Yes / No
When I do something for my husband, I expect the same in return.	Yes / No
I tend to be focused more on my needs than my husband's.	Yes / No
I was a lot more attentive to my husband when we were first married.	Yes / No
If I'm not careful I can put the needs of my job/ children/parents before my husband.	Yes / No
I paid a lot more attention to how I looked, dressed, and behaved before I was married.	Yes / No
I tend to hover when my husband is watching the kids or working on something for me.	Yes / No
I can tend to slip into "mother mode" with my husband without realizing it.	Yes / No
I can't stand to be away from my husband. I want him close by all the time.	Yes / No
I tend to do things the same every time. Spontaneity is not my strength.	Yes / No
I have a hard time letting some things go, especially if they hurt me deeply.	Yes / No
I sometimes wish my husband was more like (fill in the blank here).	Yes / No
I fantasize, at times, about an ex-boyfriend/fiancé/ husband.	Yes / No

I resent not being able to understand *why* my husband acts a certain way.	Yes / No
I am quick to point out when my husband offends me.	Yes / No
I want to "talk it out" every time something is bothering me.	Yes / No
I insist on a resolution when we talk about our issues.	Yes / No
I prefer to be silent when something is bothering me.	Yes / No
I avoid conflict by withdrawing emotionally or leaving the room.	Yes / No
I have been known to "storm out" when there is conflict.	Yes / No
I expect to be my husband's top priority, as he is mine.	Yes / No
I've said or thought the words "I've had it!" when it comes to my husband.	Yes / No
I have one or more contingencies under which I would leave the relationship.	Yes / No
I rarely consult my husband about my personal plans or dreams.	Yes / No
Because of pain in my past I am easily triggered by things my husband says to me.	Yes / No

These questions are among some I have used through the years to help identify the health of a woman's relationship with her spouse, or even her own personal emotional health. They are also questions I've had to ask myself in determining my emotional and relational health. Your responses to some statements may simply represent personality quirks or the need for further spiritual growth. However, some may indicate the presence of deeper hurts in your life or some behavior patterns you've developed from your exposure to unhealthy relationships.

If you have answered "yes" to most or all of the questions on this list, it is very likely there are perspectives and behaviors that need to be adjusted in your life. There is hope, however. The first step to transformation is recognizing the areas in which you need to change. Throughout this book, I will address many of the issues or mind-sets resulting in certain behaviors that may now be habits in your life. And I will give you tools to reverse those behaviors and start acting or responding in a way that rebuilds your relationship and recaptures your husband's heart.

As you took the quiz, did you become aware of some of the things you do that are not necessarily healthy for your relationship with your husband? Humbling, isn't it? But, as I said earlier, the first step in reversing relationship-hindering habits is to be aware of them. I will give you an opportunity to retake this self-assessment at the end of this book, and it's my prayer your answers will have changed after you've grasped tools to respond to situations differently and gained a healthier perspective of what it takes to draw your husband's heart closer to yours.

As we get started, please know this: You are not alone. I am walking alongside you through these changes I'll be asking you to make and encouraging your heart with the goal set before you. And I'll be reminding you often, as you press on for the changes you hope will take place, that there is a God alongside you too, waiting to help you experience more in your marriage.

Are you ready to get started? Then turn the page and let's start experiencing *more.*

1

Consider His Heart

Stepping Back to See the Whole Picture

Do nothing from selfishness or empty conceit,
but with humility of mind regard one another
as more important than yourselves.

PHILIPPIANS 2:3 NASB

Belinda's handwritten letter sounded desperate:

> I feel like I'm at the end of my rope. I've been married 27 years, and it's been several months since my husband and I have been intimate. He doesn't initiate ANY affection toward me, in spite of my asking. He says he still loves me and there's no one else he wants to be with and that I need to tell him what I want. I do, but still he acts like he doesn't care because he doesn't initiate holding my hand, hugging me, or kissing me. How do I remain in a marriage where there is no affection?

Sarah's e-mail to me sounded similar:

> I have a good relationship with my husband, and he tells me he is perfectly content with our marriage. But sometimes I feel like I'm lacking. I crave attention and adventure. I am fun, outgoing, and the initiator in the relationship.

> I still need romance, and he doesn't tend to need that. He makes me feel rejected at times. He's happy. I'm not.

And Debra's complaint echoed several *hundred* that I've heard in the past couple of years:

> I feel like I'm living alone in this marriage. My husband rarely talks to me about anything other than surface issues and never shares deep feelings from his heart. He's hard-working, faithful, and treats me well, but I need more. I've told him countless times what I need to feel emotionally connected to him, and he doesn't seem to care or know how to give me what I need. How much more of this can I take?

Sister, I hear you. I've walked in your shoes. I have learned, through nearly three decades of marriage—and by walking alongside many women who have expressed similar frustrations—to live by this motto when it comes to our relationships: "Marriage is not about what you are supposed to get. It's about what you were designed to *give*."

Marriage is not about what you are supposed to get but what you were designed to give.

I know that's difficult to hear when all you want is to experience more with your husband or enjoy the relationship the way it once was. But to focus on how you can *give more* in the marriage doesn't mean you give up on what you want to receive. To focus on how you can give is *the way* you begin to draw your husband's heart closer to yours and experience more trust, more passion, and more communication.

A New Motto

To start drawing your husband closer to your heart, ask not what your relationship can do for you. Ask what YOU can do for your relationship. Years of personal and counseling experience have proven that mind-set to be beneficial, and yet I know that concept rubs against our human nature, which wants to be served rather than to serve.

Several years ago, when my book *When a Woman Inspires Her Husband* was released, I received two types of responses:

1. gratitude from the women who were looking for more ways to please their husbands or excited at the prospect of being their husbands' inspiration; and
2. bitterness from the women who were incensed at the idea of another book on how to love and inspire their husbands when they felt their husbands were doing nothing to inspire or cherish them. I was asked—at least a few times, "When are you going to write a book for my husband about how *he* can inspire *me*?"

I realize now that second type of reaction was coming from women who had been wounded. Perhaps they felt they were always the ones reading the books and making the attempts to draw their husbands closer to their hearts, and they felt there was little more they could do to make a change in their marriage. It saddened me that many of the women who most needed to read about how they could inspire their husbands were unwilling to take one more step toward improving the relationship.

I can speak with credibility in this area because I've been the woman begging for—and at times bitter about—all the "more" that I believed I was entitled to. And yet, all of the talks, suggestions, and pleas with my husband to be what I wanted him to be got me nowhere. In fact, no progress was made in our relationship until I did something daring, determined, and long overdue. I stepped back to see the whole picture and considered my husband's heart.

To make progress in your relationships, you may need to do something daring, determined, and long overdue.

You and I can tend to live in the drama of us.* Our feelings, our hormones, our circumstances, our stressed schedules, and our insecurities can all affect how we see life. They are the onlookers, the bystanders in this drama of our emotions. And they might, at times, feel like the victims of whatever we unleashed on them because of what we perceived as reality.

If you and I want to draw our husbands' hearts closer and experience more with them, we need to, plain and simple, put our feelings aside and step back to see the whole picture of what is going on in our men's lives and start considering *their* hearts. As difficult as it is (myself included here), we need to take ourselves out of the equation.

A Closer Look

Let's look again at the complaints from those unhappy wives at the opening of this chapter who were hoping to experience more with their husbands. And let's see what happened as each of them began to take themselves out of the equation and consider their husband's heart.

"He Doesn't Seem to Care"

As Belinda mentioned in her letter, she felt like she was at the end of her rope because her husband didn't show affection toward her like he once did. She was frustrated. She was exhausted by all her efforts that she felt were getting her nowhere. She was exasperated because he didn't seem to care about what she needed. On the surface, it was more of a desire to have her needs met. But I think, deep inside, she truly wanted to recapture her husband's heart. She was simply going about it the wrong way. Her aim was to feel more loved, not to do what she could so that her husband felt more loved in her presence and responded accordingly.

Belinda's problem was very workable. It turned out it was more about *her response* to her husband than her husband himself.

Did you notice from her letter that within the problem there were certain positives? Belinda mentioned:

---

* Every woman knows drama, and if that is your forte—or even something you want to avoid—you might want to investigate my book *Drama Free*.

- Her husband loved her.
- There was no other woman he wanted to be with.
- He had told her to tell him what she wanted.

What was happening in Belinda's marriage was a constant cycle of expectation and disappointment, with the additional problem that one person's way of dealing with and responding to an issue was different from the other's. I think it's a cycle that all of us go through at one time or another.

After asking more questions about Belinda's situation, I discovered Belinda's husband had experienced a couple instances of male dysfunction earlier that year (something his doctor assured him was normal for a man his age). I shared with Belinda that perhaps that was all it took to shatter her husband's confidence. I asked her if it was possible that he was now fearful that his displays of affection toward her might be misinterpreted as a desire for more and thus raise her expectations, which he would worry could then result in her disappointment if he were unable to follow through. No man wants to feel like a failure in any way. Was it possible he was avoiding a situation he believed would be setting himself up for failure and her for frustration?

When Belinda considered that her husband's actions—or lack of them—could be motivated by his fear of failure, along with a concern for her (rather than an indifference to her feelings), she became more gentle and understanding toward him. She started focusing on how she could build his confidence as a man in several areas. Soon after, she noticed her husband becoming more affectionate toward her. As she extended grace and kindness toward him, he began to little by little trust her more with his affections and his words. In short, she had recaptured his heart by first considering the facts of the situation over her feelings, and then by considering his heart before her own.

"He's Happy, I'm Not"

Sarah, whose personality was more driven than her husband's, wanted to go out and grab hold of life, while he was more careful, reserved, laid-back. She saw his response to her initiation as rejection when that very likely was not his intention. It was probably more a lack of spontaneity on his part to meet her expectations. Sarah noted in her e-mail:

- She and her husband had a good relationship.
- He was perfectly content with their relationship.
- He was happy—but she was not.

Could Sarah benefit from learning what made her husband tick? Could she learn to appreciate his personality, which was more careful and methodical than hers? Could she accept the fact that he *was* motivated, he just expressed that motivation in different ways than she did?

Yes, she could. And when Sarah placed her feelings aside—and her accusation that her husband was "making" her feel a certain way—she began to understand who her husband is and why he is a certain way. When she began to focus on how she could meet *his* needs, she eventually found her husband was more responsive and was, indeed, fun to be around. She had recaptured her husband's heart and was able to experience more with him by considering the facts of the situation over her feelings, and by considering his heart before her own.

"I Feel like I'm Living Alone"

Debra, who felt her husband was not communicating intimately with her, had a spouse whom some women would die to have:

- He was hardworking.
- He was faithful.
- He treated her well—he just didn't know *how* to give her what she wanted.

Debra was expecting her husband to communicate with her at an emotional depth that he wasn't capable of—and might not ever be. But Debra was having difficulty defining to me—and to her husband—what "depth of communication" really looked like to her.

"I want to know what's on his heart, what he thinks about, what he longs for," she said. Debra's husband was clearly at a loss for how to put that into words and therefore give Debra what she wanted. As Debra removed her expectations and demands from the scenario, she began to see that her husband was a deep thinker who processed situations internally rather than verbally expressing his frustrations, desires, or dreams. She also discovered that her husband had many characteristics worth praising. She began to wonder if he rarely communicated verbally out of fear of being judged by her for his lack of "depth." She realized it was not fair of her to complain about her husband's personality differences when he was, in fact, the man she married and promised to love unconditionally, even if she discovered later that he processed life differently from her.

Debra, too, was able to experience more with her husband when she started accepting him as the man God made him and considering his heart before her own.

Is removing one's expectations a matter of settling? No. It's a matter of accepting reality and making the best of it. It's an exercise in unconditional love. And it's a necessary part of considering your husband's heart so you can eventually recapture it.

Removing one's expectations is an exercise in unconditional love.

The Positives Within the Problem

You've heard it said, "In every cloud, there's a silver lining." I would venture to say, "In every problem, there is a positive...or a situation for which we can be grateful." Each of the women I mentioned felt her relationship and her husband were lacking in some way. But when each took herself out of the equation and looked at the situation from the standpoint of love—grabbing hold of the good points and remembering that the heart of her husband really was to please her—she gained the ability to show grace and understanding, and eventually saw her marriage improve.

In every problem there is a positive.

Each of the wives we looked at was originally concentrating on how she *felt* in her situation. And feelings can deceive us every time. Our feelings can distort the facts. They can lead to improper conclusions. Feelings can muddy the water in marriage. These wives needed to consider the facts of their situations. Their husbands were different from them, they processed life differently, they had their own fears and concerns—and hurting their wives was not even on their radar. Sometimes we have to take our feelings out of the equation to see the facts more clearly and respond appropriately.

Is your husband failing to meet your expectations in some way? Then it may be time to put your feelings aside, dial down the expectations, and step back to get a bird's-eye view of the situation. Lest it sound like I am unsympathetic with the issues you are dealing with, let me tell you how I immediately related to Debra's story.

My Experience with Silence

For years my husband, who is a pastor, believed it was better not to talk to me about what bothered him about his job because he didn't want me to share the weight that was burdening him. It was his way of protecting me. Yet I was feeling punished instead—feeling shut out, feeling he was angry with me, and feeling he was not letting me into his heart. A simple resolution to my hurt feelings, in my thinking, would have been for him to communicate that he was troubled by something concerning his work, even if he didn't want to share all the details.

In fact, if I could've written the script for him, it would've been worded like this:

> Cindi, I'm troubled by a situation I'm dealing with at work. It has nothing to do with you and me, but please trust me when I say it's best if I don't share it with you or trouble you with it. Right now I just need your understanding and I need you to trust my wisdom when I'm being silent.

Would you believe I actually *did* write that out for him and hand it to him and ask him to recite it to me when the situation called for it? (I know, I've had my controlling issues to deal with too.) His response was a look that said, "You're kidding, right?" and then he smiled and said, "Yeah, what you wrote? That's pretty much it. Why don't you keep that in a place where you can pull it out and read it the next time I'm acting moody and you don't understand why?"

Would I have preferred that he just learn to lovingly say it? You bet. But is that reality? No. My husband is who he is. He processes life and problems and concerns mostly internally and silently, not always by verbally extending to me so that I have confidence that we are still emotionally connected.

In all fairness, Hugh has learned through the years to talk more about how he is feeling and what he is going through. At times his talking comes across as "venting," and I have to be careful not to take it personally or suggest, in the middle of his venting, how he could better communicate his feelings. When Hugh opens up, he doesn't need a lecture on how to better communicate. He needs to be heard and understood. I've learned that a time of listening, followed by nodding and a tender word or two (and that's it!), are the reactions he needs and prefers.

Rather than insisting my husband begin to handle things in a way that fits my need for communication, I had to, years ago, take myself out of the equation and remove the expectation that he will say certain words to relieve my fears that he is upset with me. I extended grace and decided to understand the ways he is different from me and do what he needs most: love and accept him for who he is.

Isn't that what each of us truly needs in our relationships? Isn't that what we long for? Isn't that the basis for intimacy? To be loved as we are?

To be unconditionally accepted in spite of our inadequacies and failure to act or respond according to another's expectations?

That is how we are loved by God—unconditionally and in spite of our failures and inadequacies. And that is how God expects us to love our husbands. Unconditionally. And in spite of their failures and inadequacies. It's difficult at times. But it's necessary if we want to remove the baggage, rebuild love, and experience more with our husbands.

God's Example to Us

God gave us a picture of unconditional love in a passage that is often quoted at weddings:

> Love is patient, love is kind. It does not envy, it does not boast, it is not proud. It does not dishonor others, it is not self-seeking, it is not easily angered, it keeps no record of wrongs. Love does not delight in evil but rejoices with the truth. It always protects, always trusts, always hopes, always perseveres (1 Corinthians 13:4-7).

How can you and I be patient and kind if we don't take ourselves out of the equation? How can we refrain from being envious, boastful, proud, or rude unless we've put our own feelings aside and considered our husbands' hearts? How do we not become easily angered and how do we keep no record of wrongs? We remove ourselves and consider someone else in our place. Jesus called it dying to self.

Throughout the New Testament we are exhorted to die to ourselves and our sin and selfish ways and let Christ live through us.[1] So what is the Bible's definition of love in 1 Corinthians 13 and what does the Bible instruct us to do when it comes to our relationships? We are to die to ourselves. We are to take ourselves out of the equation and serve the other.

In Philippians 2:3-4 we are told:

> Do nothing from selfishness or empty conceit, but with humility of mind regard one another as more important than yourselves; do not merely look out for your own personal interests, but also for the interests of others (NASB).

One way you and I can apply this passage in the Bible to our marriages is to think about how our husbands might be struggling right now to meet *our* needs. Think back to the day when your husband was able to meet your needs. It was probably during a time when you were most likely meeting a lot of *his* needs too. What has changed since then? Can you start, from this point forward, loving your husband for who he is and remembering why you entered into this relationship in the first place? Can you begin to focus on what you can give to improve his life, instead of what you can get from him to improve yours? We all tend to start our relationships focused on the other person, but how quickly our focus narrows back to ourselves.

Take yourself out of the equation and start practicing understanding, grace, and unconditional love. It is what God did for you when He sent His Son to this earth to die for your sins...to, in a sense, take care of a mess you could never begin to deal with. And all that God asks in return is that you die to self (as He died for you) and trust Him with your life, your soul, your marriage. Can you do that? Of course you can. (For more on what it means to surrender your life and marriage to Christ, see "Dying to Self in Your Marriage" on page 193.)

Putting Yourself on the Shelf

Jesus modeled to us unconditional love when He wrestled with His Father over His impending death on the cross to pay the penalty for your sins and mine. In His heartfelt prayer in the middle of the night, Jesus cried out, "Father, if You are willing, remove this cup from Me; yet not My will, but Yours be done" (Luke 22:42 NASB).

It was the ultimate surrender of His life for ours. It was God's will that Jesus complete the task He came to this earth for...that life of full obedience to His Father be culminated in His sacrificial death on the cross to pay the penalty for our sins so that we could live eternally with Him. Nowhere is there a more perfect example of surrender than in that prayer in which Jesus gave up what He feared and felt for what He knew had to be done to secure our forever. He was sealing our "happily ever after" with Him when He died on that cross and then rose again from the dead three days later. But that seal of our forever started with the forfeit of His own will.

That is a beautiful example to us of how marriage should work and how we can seal our "till death do us part" with our spouse.

In our book *When Couples Walk Together*, Hugh and I included a chapter called "Leaving Self on the Shelf" and offered suggestions of practical ways that you and your husband can die to self and thereby honor one another. There is no more direct way to draw your husband's heart toward yours than to put yourself on the shelf and echo Jesus' words, "Not my will, but yours." Here are some ways you can do that:

- Not my feelings to protect tonight, but yours.
- Not my night to have uninterrupted sleep, but yours.
- Not my turn to have the last say, but yours.
- Not my dream to pursue right now, but yours.
- Not my time to dominate the conversation, but yours.
- Not my place to point out your mistake, but your place to feel loved.
- Not my time to feel sorry for myself, but your time to receive grace.
- Not my needs that are of utmost importance right now, but yours.

Those words become easier to think—and actually say—when our hearts are aligned with God's heart for our husbands. You may have reasons for thinking ill of your spouse, but having a loving mind-set for your husband like God has for you will make acceptance, compassion, and forgiveness more forthcoming than accusation, complaint, and frustration.

Back to the Basics

Every relationship needs do-overs or fresh starts. Here's yours. Go back to the basics by following these ABCs. They will help you take yourself out of the equation and love your spouse selflessly.

A—Accept That Your Husband Cannot Meet All Your Emotional Needs

Your husband was not meant to fulfill you in every way. You must find your acceptance, security, sense of worth, and identity in who God says you are. As you begin to see who you are in the eyes of your Creator and heavenly Father, you will gain the kind of confidence that exudes beauty and elicits pursuit. Even if your man doesn't follow suit, you will have done what you needed to do to be more able and stable to deal with whatever comes (or doesn't come) your way. (For more on how to draw closer to God and see Him as your spiritual Husband who can meet all your needs, thereby freeing up your spouse from your emotional expectations, see my book *Letting God Meet Your Emotional Needs.*)

B—Be the Helper He Needs You to Be

In Genesis 2:18, we see that God designed woman to be man's "helper." When our focus shifts to "how can my husband help me?"—and we insist on being needed, appreciated, encouraged, and affirmed—we are no longer helping. We are clinging—and in some ways *crippling*—our husbands. Personally, I have found that I am far more fulfilled when I am focusing on being my husband's helper and companion than when I'm being his complainer and crippler.

I am far more fulfilled when I am focusing on being my husband's helper and companion than when I'm being his complainer and crippler.

C—Consider Your Husband's Needs Above Your Own

This isn't novel advice. Jesus Himself said it in so many words when He told us to pick up our crosses and follow Him. That basically means we must die to ourselves. As we die to our needs in the relationship, we model Christ's love to our spouse and, in a sense, we are saying to him what Christ would: "I will sacrifice for you. I will love you unconditionally. I will be there for you to the end, regardless of your mistakes."

We've been told that kind of love isn't healthy. That it's tolerating. That it's enabling. But taking ourselves out of the equation isn't enabling, it's *empowering.* It is how we love another as God loves us.

Taking ourselves out of the equation isn't enabling, it's empowering.

PRAYING IT THROUGH

Incorporating the ABCs and loving your husband as I just described isn't easy at times. In fact, it's not even human. It's godly. And it takes the strength of God, through His Holy Spirit, to enable any one of us to love selflessly like that.

So let's elicit God's help right now by praying this prayer together:

> *God, I do not have it in me to love my husband as You expect me to, as I've been called to do, as I once promised to. But with Your help I can do anything. Please love my spouse through me. Consume me with Your thoughts for him so that I think only the best of him and am ready to show grace, understanding, and love even when my needs aren't being met. When I begin to think I'm being treated unfairly, or I'm giving more than I'm receiving, switch my focus back to what You did for me and help me mirror that kind of unconditional, sacrificial love toward him. Please open my husband's eyes to see my heart going after his, and may he recognize that I am loving him as You love him. Use that, Lord God, to align his heart more closely with mine.*

YOUR FOCUS FOR THE WEEK

Take yourself out of the equation this week by picking a few of the phrases on page 26 to say to your husband when appropriate.

In addition, write a few more here that will help you put yourself on the shelf and consider his heart above your own:

-

-

-

And if you haven't yet surrendered your life and marriage to Christ, won't you take that step now? I'd be happy to walk you through that process on page 193.

2

Think It Through

Renewing Your Mind to Respond like a New Wife

How much more pleasing
is your love than wine.
SONG OF SONGS 4:10

In the introduction to this book I shared a worn letter I found in my dresser drawer, penned by my husband just a few months after our wedding. I also found another such gem, one that reminded me—from my husband's words 25 years ago—of the new wife he still had four years into our marriage:

> *Cindi:*
>
> *Thank you so much for your commitment to our marriage. You always notice when our relationship needs an extra boost to keep its intensity alive. And I always notice your concern to keep our marriage moving forward.*
>
> *Thanks for being patient with me as I learn and grow in our relationship. Keep in mind that I've never been a husband before—everything I am learning is on a first-time basis. This is also the longest relationship I've ever had and the one I've enjoyed the most—that is something that cannot change.*

My love, my respect, and my gratitude for you have all continued to increase since we fell in love. I love you above all created things, Beloved.

Your Forever Man,
Hugh

Wow. What was I doing back then to show commitment to our marriage that caused such appreciation by him? As I thought long and hard about it, I came up with the answer. I was responding to him like a new wife.

The New-Wife Mind-set

Remember when you were a new wife? It might be decades ago or just a few weeks. But, oh, what a feeling! You couldn't wait until you got off work (or until he got off work) so the two of you could be together again. You constantly checked your voice mail messages or your phone to see if he had called during the day. You had a special sparkle in your eyes when you talked of him and a spring in your step when you walked alongside him. You were excited at just the thought of being in his presence. (By the way, if that's where you are right now—you go, girl! Don't *ever* lose that. And read on to make sure you don't.)

There is a beautiful song in Scripture that describes young love. It sings of romantic love, exciting love, passionate love. It is the "wedding song" of King Solomon—the son of David and Bathsheba—to his bride, a simple Jewish maiden whom Scripture calls "the Shulamite woman." This song has been divided into eight chapters and given chapter headings and verse numbers, and now it reads in Scripture like a narrative. But it's definitely a song. It's one of the most beautiful love songs that exists. In this song, it's as if God pulled back the curtain to give us an up-close look at intimacy done right.

In this moving song, drama, and poem, King Solomon and his bride describe in intimate detail their feelings for each other and their longings to be together. This song contains the most explicit statements on sex in the Bible. But it remains pure, innocent, undefiled, and a part of the inspired Word of God. That means God's smile of approval is on every stanza.

The song stresses the themes of love and devotion between a husband and a wife who are committed to each other, while also echoing the loving relationship between God and His people Israel and between Christ and His church.[1]

One commentator said, "The Song is a convincing witness that men and women were created physically, emotionally, and spiritually to live in love. At the outset of Scripture we read, 'It is not good for man to live alone' (Genesis 2:18). The Song of Songs elaborates on the Genesis story by celebrating the union of two diverse personalities in love."[2] Two *diverse* personalities. Did you catch that? That is true of your marriage too: Your husband who is unlike you in many ways, and you, whom God has brought to his side.

This song might sound like love that you experienced at one time. Or it might express an intensity you still dream about. But regardless of where you are in your relationship with your husband, you can experience this kind of love with *him*. (And I'm going to guess it's the kind of love your husband is dying to experience with *you* too.)

Solomon's song to his bride is called the Song of Songs or "The Best Song." And when you think about it, if the events of your life were recorded as songs, couldn't your first few memories of being engaged and married be considered by both of you as "The Best Song"?

Learning from The Song

In the next several chapters I'll refer to portions of this song and go into depth on a few of the points. For now, let's look at an overview of this new bride's response to her husband. Let's focus on what we can glean from a wife who is very much in love and gain insights as to why she is so cherished by her beloved.

1. *She delights in his love.* This song opens with Solomon's bride saying, "Let him kiss me with the kisses of his mouth—for your love is better than wine" (Song of Songs 1:2 NKJV). Wine is a metaphor for pleasure, intoxication,

sweetness, and exhilaration, thus this expression suggests that this woman's love of her beloved brought her indescribable and incomparable joy and delight.[3] *Does just knowing you are loved by your husband bring you great joy?*

2. *She loves his scent and the sound of his name.* In the very next verse, she says, "Pleasing is the fragrance of your perfumes; your name is like perfume poured out. No wonder the young women love you!" (Song of Songs 1:3). You could say she loved everything about him—the smell of his clothing, the scent of his skin, the sound of his name. In fact, the mere mention of his name aroused in her pleasurable thoughts and great affection. *How do you say your husband's name? In an exasperated tone? Or is it an endearment to you?*

3. *She longs to know the details of his day.* "Tell me, you whom I love, where you graze your flock and where you rest your sheep at midday" (Song of Songs 1:7). In *The Message* this passage reads, "Tell me where you're working—I love you so much—Tell me where you're tending your flocks, where you let them rest at noontime. Why should I be the one left out, outside the orbit of your tender care?" This bride wanted to know where her husband was, not out of suspicion, but because she longed to know what he was doing and how his day was going. He occupied her thoughts. *Do you think of your husband throughout the day, wondering how that meeting went, what he's encountering, where he ate lunch, and how he's doing? Do you show an interest in his everyday life and job?*

4. *She returns his compliments.* Solomon was adoring of his bride and heaped compliments upon her. But instead of a shy "thank you" or a denial because she disagreed with her husband's compliment (how many times do we do that, girls?), she returned the compliment and talked of how

stunning he was: "How handsome you are, my beloved! Oh, how charming!" (Song of Songs 1:16). Granted, this is much easier to do when your husband is doting on you. Even still, *do you often tell your husband how handsome—or hot—he is?*

5. *She focuses on his uniqueness.* In the first half of Song 2:3, Solomon's bride says, "Like an apple tree among the trees of the forest is my beloved among the young men." It's clear here that her husband was taller than the other men. She delighted in the way he "stood out from the crowd." Do you see your husband as ten feet tall, even if he's not? It's easy for you and me to compare our husbands to others and maybe even focus on how they fall short. But in what ways does he stand out? In what areas is he smarter, sharper, more experienced, unique? *Can you let him know that you see him as "taller" than he actually is?*

6. *She longs to be with him.* In the second half of Song 2:3, this new bride says, "All I want is to sit in his shade, to taste and savor his delicious love" (MSG). In Song 3:1-3, she even gets up in the middle of the night and looks for him because she longs for his presence right beside her. True love involves "pain in separation." The Shulamite bride was in pain when her lover was not around. *Do you long to be with your husband so much it hurts when he is away?*

7. *She feels protected by his love.* In Song 2:4, she says, "He brought me to the banqueting house; and his banner over me was love." Here she was describing how his love for her helped her feel protected and at ease. There is a comfort expressed here in their sexual relationship, which is huge to a man. A man feels like a man when he knows his wife enjoys him (physically and sexually) and feels protected by his strength and love for her. *Can you let your husband know how safe you feel in his arms and by knowing he loves you intimately?*

8. *She anticipates his arrival with great joy.* I love the way *The Message* translates Song 2:8-10, the Shulamite's song of her husband's arrival. Listen to her voice, giddy and expectant, as she described her husband from a distance:

   Look? Listen? There's my lover!
   Do you see him coming?
   Vaulting the mountains,
   leaping the hills.
   My lover is like a gazelle, graceful;
   like a young stag, virile.
   Look at him there, on tiptoe at the gate,
   all ears, all eyes—ready!
   My lover has arrived
   and he's speaking to me!

   Can you imagine what your greeting would be like if you were this excited to see your husband every time he walked through the door? Can you imagine how much earlier he might come home, knowing this was what awaited him? This bride surely let her husband know he was king of the castle (which he literally was). *How can you let your husband feel like a king when he walks through the door?*

9. *She seeks to "catch" what is causing conflict between them and rid the house of it.* Song 2:15 says, "Catch us the foxes, the little foxes that spoil the vines, for our vines have tender grapes" (NKJV). "Foxes that spoil the vines" is a reference to small pests or intruders that were a common problem for vineyard keepers.[4]

   Every marriage has "little foxes" in the form of problems, differences, or irritations that can run through the marriage and cause conflict. This bride recognized the need to catch them right away so they weren't allowed to *live* with them and continue to wreak havoc in their vineyard (another word for marriage or sexual experience). She also recognized that what they had was tender, and she was not willing to let anything spoil it. *Can you be devoted to catching whatever runs through your marriage and seeks to destroy it?*

10. *She recognizes they belong to one another.* Long before the apostle Paul instructed the Ephesians that when they married they were one body and belonged to one another (Ephesians 5:21-33), this young bride sang, "My beloved is mine and I am his" (Song of Songs 2:16). She was echoing the Genesis 2:24 proclamation and command that the husband and wife are "one flesh." She was able to sense, in this gift of love, that he was hers and she was his, which led to a generosity toward one another sexually as well as sacrificially. How could any man not desire a woman who considers her body his own and his body hers? *Can you start treating your body like a gift for your husband and help take care of his body as if it were an extension of your own? (Because, according to the Word of God, it is!)*

How could any man not desire a woman who considers her body his own and his body hers?

---

11. *She invites him to find pleasure in her.* "Let my beloved come into his garden and taste its choice fruits" (Song of Songs 4:16). Here, this young, obviously confident bride invited her husband to find pleasure in her. There is nothing more appealing to a husband than for his own wife to initiate lovemaking, and that happens when you and I are confident in who we are, confident we are loved, and confident we won't be rejected. Unless your husband has repeatedly turned down your advances and there are other related issues that need to be addressed first, then, *invite him willingly to find pleasure in you.*

12. *She repents and initiates reconciliation when she realizes she's been complacent.* In Song 5:2-8 (go ahead, get out your Bible and read it!), we see the beginning of what looks like "everyday life." Had the honeymoon worn off? Was she used to having him around? We see that he came to her, but she'd locked her door (closed off her heart, didn't see or hear him, wasn't interested).

    In every marriage, complacency sets in. We get tired, bored, or just plain uninterested in our sexual relationship. We sometimes even begin to have excuses for why we don't want to be intimate, why we don't feel like talking, and why we don't even want to be close to our husbands. One commentator said this of the passage: "Every relationship experiences periods of apathy or indifference. However, the Shulamite did not remain in that state but repents (v. 6–8), had a reawakening of her affections for her lover (v. 10–16) and changed her heart, leading to reconciliation (Song of Songs 6:1–13)."[5] You and I might often realize that something needs to change in the relationship or a problem needs to be dealt with. Can we do it graciously, admitting our part in what went wrong so we can turn things back around? A husband who knows his wife is eager to reconcile is a husband who will not hesitate to admit when he is wrong. *Can you be the one to initiate reconciliation?**

A husband who knows his wife is eager to reconcile is a husband who will not hesitate to admit when he is wrong.

---

* I'm thinking you *already are* the one who initiates reconciliation because, after all, YOU are the one reading a book about how to experience more in your relationship with him. Good job!

13. *She allows him to admire her beauty.* In Song 7:1-9, Solomon gives a detailed description of his bride from the sandals on her feet to the hair on top of her head. Some commentators believe she might have been dancing before him as he compiled this description. Now, you might be thinking, *If I were a young bride with a lean, flat stomach and looked like her, yeah, I'd dance before my husband.* Perhaps you aren't comfortable with your husband inspecting you from head to toe. Or maybe he's made a remark in the past that has you feeling self-conscious. I realize it is ingrained in us by our culture (and perhaps by some past wounds of yours) not to be an "object" before any man and to be offended at any reference to your body being a point of visual pleasure for your husband. Yet please remember something: You are his for life, and you are the only woman he can gaze upon and enjoy with a right heart before God. If he looks at anyone else the way he is allowed by God to look at you, he will be committing lust and adultery in his heart. *So let him feast his eyes on you. Allow him to enjoy what he sees by taking the best care of yourself that you can, by dressing nicely, smelling nicely, and looking at him with the eyes you once had for him.* Perhaps as you begin to look at him the way you once did, he will return that look the way *he* once did. (Stick with me, I'll address this more thoroughly in chapter 7.)

Perhaps as you begin to look at him the way you once did, he will return that look the way he *once did.*

---

14. *She plans sensual pleasures for her husband.* In Song 7:13, the bride sings, "The mandrakes [an herb known to aid in fertility] send out their fragrance, and at our door is every

delicacy, both new and old, that I have stored up for you, my beloved." She was planning ways to please him, both sexually and otherwise. One commentator said, "The Shulamite had planned sensual pleasures carefully for her beloved. She would give her love to him in ways new and old."[6] *What do YOU have stored up for your husband?*

15. *She desires permanence and security from him.* "Place me as a seal upon your heart, like a seal on your arm; for love is as strong as death...Many waters cannot quench love; rivers cannot sweep it away" (Song of Songs 8:6-7). The seal was a mark of ownership and official commitment. This woman wanted to be a "seal" upon her lover's heart because the nearness to the seat of his affection gave her security. She wanted to be a "seal" upon his arm to remind her of his protection and strength. The phrase "as strong as death" suggested the finality and immutability of his love. The reference to jealousy was a reminder of the exclusive intensity of his love that could be described as a "waterproof torch."[7] *Do you let your husband know that nothing can diminish, drown, or destroy the love you have for him?*

Do you let your husband know that nothing can diminish, drown, or destroy the love you have for him?

In chapter 11, we will look at a "stick it out" mind-set that might be one of the most important things you can do to endear yourself to your husband's heart. It's far too easy for husbands and wives today to look at marriage as something that will only last "as long as we both shall love." But God's intention for your union is that it last your lifetime—or his—as long as you both shall *live.* This woman saw their love as permanent, unable to be changed by life's circumstances. When your husband sees that "many waters cannot quench love, nor can the floods drown it," he will have no excuse but to trust you with his life, his commitment, his secrets, and his words.

I can't help but think this exchange between a husband and wife is an example of what God designed for us throughout our married life—not just for the first few weeks or years of our marriage. This woman was in love, and it is so evident by how she spoke to and about her husband, and how she longed for him. Oh, to always have that passion and fervor. But we also see something else implied. Her husband was enraptured by her. And it wasn't just because she was young and pretty, girls. We will look more at this in chapter 7, but for now let's focus on her response to him. This is how a new bride—a young woman in love—acts and talks. *What man wouldn't want to be in the presence of a woman who adores him and wants him for life?*

Wait a Minute!

Now, I can guess what you might be thinking: *Sure, Cindi, she responds that way because they just got married. Love is new. But what about years later, when some of the baggage sets in? What about when the kids come, and finances are tight, and the job demands everything, and an aging parent moves in or passes away? What about when life happens and the marital bliss becomes a distant memory? How do you respond like a new wife then?*

I do wish the Song of Songs contained another couple of chapters that showed us if the Shulamite bride was as good of a wife when she became a mom! It would be nice to know if she continued to praise her husband after she saw the mistakes he made (like years later when he amassed more than 900 wives and 300 concubines!). It would've been nice to know where those two were at the *end* of their lives together, and not just the beginning.

Yet I can't help but think that this song encompasses more than just the first few weeks or months of marriage. I think it represents *seasons* of married life in which we're not that interested sexually, not that vested emotionally, not that passionate about the relationship.

In chapter 5 of the Song of Songs, when he knocked on her door at night (verse 2), I don't believe the reason she wouldn't get out of bed to let him in was that she had taken off her robe and didn't want to put it back on or had washed her feet and didn't want to get them dirty again (as she claimed in verse 3). I believe it was because they'd been married awhile and sex wasn't quite as exciting, and she'd rather have her rest than accommodate his desire for pleasure. I think we can even apply that incident to days when we're exhausted from work, or weeks that we're consumed with a project, or years that we're worn out from raising kids or working toward the promotion or caregiving for our aging parents. I think it applies to those times when you finally put your head on your pillow and he wants to do WHAT? But then, further in the song, she goes after him, and she regrets having missed the opportunity to be with him. There was then restoration, and she was singing his praises again by the sixth chapter, which I'd like to think occurred toward the end of their lives.

Regardless of the time frame, we can apply this to our lives and how we respond to our husbands *throughout* our lives. Because how *our* love story continues or ends is in many ways dependent on the choices you and I make from day to day.

In the next chapter I'm going to address some of those issues that slow the passion, primarily how to still put our husbands first after the kids come, after we have our dream job, after we've grown used to each other, after the transitions and struggles of life come our way. But for now, I want us to reflect on the primary reason we don't continue to see our husbands as our beloved bridegroom.

Conformed to Our Culture

Certainly, after 30 years with my husband, there have been times I've stopped acting like a new wife. Partly because I wasn't being deliberate and intentional in responding lovingly to my husband, but also because I unknowingly let the culture around me redefine marriage from a covenant and commitment to a convenience.

Without realizing it you and I can let our hopes, dreams, and ideas of marriage melt into a pessimistic "this is reality" mind-set and then we start seeing our marriage like the world without God sees it.

Scripture exhorts us in Romans 12:2: "Do not conform to the

pattern of this world, but be transformed by the renewing of your mind. Then you will be able to test and approve what God's will is—his good, pleasing and perfect will." To not conform to the pattern of this world, we need to make sure our perspective on marriage aligns with the Word of God, not the world without God.

I'm sure you know what I'm talking about. Think back to your wedding day and the vows you recited and the weeks surrounding that blissful day. It was you and your husband on top of the world, wasn't it? You felt unstoppable, didn't you? You were young, in love, and starting out with the man of your dreams.

You were optimistic: *We are going to have a beautiful life together.* You were determined: *There's nothing we can't do together!* You were spiritual: *God has brought the two of us together for His purposes!* You were grateful: *I'm so fortunate to have him.* And you were fierce: *We will never be apart. We will withstand the tests of time. Nothing can stop us now.*

Were you and I simply being idealistic? Or had we caught God's vision for our union? Were we young and naïve? Or were we reveling in God's blessing in our life and not letting anything else affect our gratitude for what we'd been given?

When we get married nearly all of us believe that God brought our man to us and we are blessed among women! Then our perspective starts changing as we stop focusing on what we've been *given* and we start complaining about what we aren't *getting*. Simply said, we start thinking and acting *unlike* a new wife.

Marriage is not about what you and I can get out of the relationship; it's about what we can give in the relationship. It isn't a 50-50 arrangement, meaning we each compromise so none of us is putting forth more effort than the other. It is a 100-100 arrangement; we each give 100 percent. Marriage isn't about personal happiness, and it isn't meant to last "as long as you both shall love." It's about personal *holiness* and conforming both of you to the image of Christ—as long as you both shall *live* (Romans 8:28-29).

When you spoke vows to each other before God and witnesses, God put a seal on you and your husband's unity that He intends to keep unbreakable as you each surrender your marriage to Him. I hope that gives you confidence in the union you have with your husband. And I hope it reminds you that you have an Ally when it comes to your desire of wanting to experience more with your husband.

WORKING IT THROUGH

The only way you and I will not be conformed to this culture's views on marriage is if we renew our minds to think differently, as Romans 12:2 commands. Then, that verse says, we will be able to test and approve what God's will is—His good, pleasing, and perfect will.

I truly want to be able to test and approve God's will—and experience His good, pleasing, and perfect will—in my marriage. Therefore, I will allow myself to be transformed by God through the renewing of my mind to think and respond like a new bride. Will you join me? When you and I start responding to our husbands the way we used to, we may soon find our husbands responding to us the way *they* once did.

YOUR FOCUS FOR THE WEEK

We looked at 15 actions, attitudes, and responses of the new bride on pages 33-40. Choose at least three of them to focus on this week (and list them below) so that your husband feels like he has a *brand-new wife*—you!

-
-
-

3

Keep Him First

Prioritizing Him Above Everyone Else

My beloved is mine and I am his.

SONG OF SONGS 2:16

Judy remembers when she was "totally poured into the kids." And so does her husband, Monte.

Judy never really thought about trying to look pretty for him or dressing cute or going out with him while she was being a mom to their two boys.

"I didn't overlook him intentionally," Judy said. "I was just so focused on our two sons. All that time, Monte sat in the background."

Judy would have continued to unknowingly put her children above her marriage, but fortunately Monte intervened.

About eight years ago, Monte learned that his friend at work had separated from his wife right after their only son left home for college. The friend explained that they had stayed together for the sake of their son until he was grown. When Monte heard that, he started thinking, *I don't want that to happen to us.* He was *determined* not to let that happen to them. So he started suggesting to his wife that they do things together again like go out to dinner, see a movie, and get out of town for the weekend.

Shortly after, they took a trip to Palm Springs.

"It was there we hit a turning point in our marriage," Judy said. "We got into our hotel room, and he handed me this huge bag. In it were clothes he had purchased for me. I remember thinking they were kind of sexy clothes that I would've never bought for myself. They weren't inappropriate or immodest or anything, just form-fitting, tighter, actually much more attractive than anything I'd ever worn.

"I immediately tried on a tight, whitewashed denim miniskirt with a fringed hem. I was not a slender woman by any means back then. And yet he loved the way the skirt looked on me. And the funny thing is, I loved it too.

"My jaw hit the floor when I saw how I could look…so much more attractive than I had been looking, simply because of how I had been choosing to dress. I never realized how frumpy I'd become. I'd wear floral, baggy capris, baggy shirts, nothing form-fitting, nothing even cute. Just frumpy. I was so into mom mode that when I saw something cute on a rack or on a mannequin I would just think, *That's for other women, younger women, women who aren't moms.* My desire for comfort had taken over, and I forgot I was a wife!

"Monte admitted he was very nervous at what my reaction would be. He hoped his gesture wouldn't backfire. He loved me no matter what I looked like and no matter how I dressed, but he wanted me to know I would look great in those clothes. And actually, I was flattered."

That became a turning point for Judy and Monte. Not only did she become aware that her husband still wanted her attention and shouldn't have to compete with their children to get it, but she also started buying clothes that actually looked good on her, that she knew he'd like, instead of just what she thought was comfortable.

Once Judy started dating her husband again, wearing more attractive clothes, and feeling better about how she looked, she also started taking better care of herself through a better diet and a more active lifestyle. Over the next several years she lost about 30 pounds.

Today Judy stays active by exercising four to five days a week and eats well. Their two sons are grown and out of the house now, and she and Monte are one of the happiest, healthiest, and closest couples I know. I met Judy for lunch just recently, and she was wearing a short white skirt with a burgundy V-neck top. She looked darling, yet modest, and years younger than her age. She had a glow about her—a confident glow that comes from knowing she is a woman much loved.

Fortunately for both of them, Monte witnessed his wife transition from a mother back into a lover.

Mark, however, wasn't as fortunate.

All About the Kids

I remember having a conversation with Mark's wife, Samantha. She was busy running her four kids here and there for their after-school activities, working on her master's degree, and working long hours as a real estate agent to help ease the family's financial stress. She mentioned to me over lunch that she and her husband hadn't exchanged more than a few words with each other all week.

"We barely have time to talk anymore," she said. "And when we do it all revolves around the kids—where they are, what they need, how they're doing in school, and who will take which one where."

"Oh, Sam, that's not good," I said. "Try to start making time for date nights once in a while, so the two of you can spend some quality time together. Move things in your schedule if you must because if you don't make the effort now to stay connected with him, emotionally and physically, by the time your last kid leaves the house, you and your husband will be strangers. You won't have anything to talk about anymore."

Her response surprised and scared me. "I don't know if I'm still going to be around by then," she said.

Fast-forward six years. Samantha ended up moving out not when their fourth child left home but when their *first* one did. When I sat across the table from her shortly after she left her husband, I asked her what went wrong. But part of me already knew the answer.

"We were going two different directions," she said. "We grew apart. I feel like I don't even know him anymore."

Sometimes we can invest so much of our time and energy into our children's lives that we don't know who our husbands are anymore.

The next time I saw Mark he told Hugh and me what he thought went wrong in his marriage.

"I believe it all goes back to when our fourth child was born," he said.

"We went from a relationship to a partnership." Mark explained that he and Samantha, like all couples, started out enjoying each other in a *romantic* relationship and eventually ended up *enduring* each other in what felt like a business partnership.

"When we started developing different priorities and investing our lives in our kids—instead of in each other—it was only a matter of time before we were in different places relationally, and quite a distance apart."

When they began to focus on what the children needed over what their marriage needed, Mark's and Sam's lives were no longer about each other and what originally brought them together.

Mark summed it up with sadness and regret: "Our lives eventually consisted of driving the kids around, delegating responsibilities, managing debt, and ultimately dividing our assets."

Don't Do It

Your career, your children, your parents, your hobbies—they can each add an extra dimension and challenge to marriage, especially if you start putting them before your husband. When you are starting out, you think that when you have a baby your love will be complete, you'll be a family, you will have even more to love and more love for each other. And you think that when you or your spouse gets the dream job, you'll have more money and be able to do with your spouse all that you want to do. But transitions, like raising children, job promotions, career changes, even having to care for aging parents, bring additional demands and responsibilities, tighter schedules, more costs, and increased stress. You begin to feel like it won't be until you have an empty house again or when you're enjoying being grandparents that you will finally be able to remember what it was like to be newlyweds.

Whether it's your children, your stepchildren, your parents, your in-laws, your job, or your finances, don't let them sap you of the energy your husband still wants and needs from you. Don't allow anything to start coming between the two of you. Be deliberate and intentional about putting your marriage first so your husband always knows he's a priority.

Don't let anything sap you of the energy your husband still wants and needs from you.

What Would a "New Bride" Do?

As I said in chapter 2, I wish the Bible had revisited the story of Solomon and his bride later in life—at least after they started having kids. It would have been great to see how Mrs. Solomon related to her husband then—and if she continued to look at him like a young bride or if the years and the mileage had muddied her view of him. Did they fall out of love because she got too involved in the kids' lives and it wasn't all about Solomon anymore? Did they grow distant because he put his work first and she let him? Did she develop a group of girlfriends she hung out with and felt more connected with than her husband? And if she was able to maintain those affections for him, it would've been nice to learn some principles from how she responded to him. Culturally, marriage was seen back then so differently than it is today. We tend to move ourselves into the equation so much that we have to constantly remind ourselves that we live with a person we promised to put first and love until the day we die.

It's quite easy to act like a new bride when you *are* a new bride or before you have children, or teenagers, or grown kids with teenagers! What I found as I interviewed wives for this book is that many of them didn't start acting like young brides again until the kids were grown and gone and they had the house to themselves. Or until they retired and no one else was vying for their time.

How can you and I still respond to our husbands like new wives when we *do* have kids? How can we keep our marriages fresh even though we're dealing with stress? How do you experience more with your husband when everyone else is competing for your time? The short answer is *keep him first.*

First Things First

Now, when I say *keep him first* I don't mean above your relationship with God, of course. Your relationship with God must come first in order for you to have the strength and love to be the kind of wife you need to be. But when it comes to other people or priorities, including children, your husband needs to know he is your first earthly priority. Otherwise he will feel last.

Your husband needs to know he is your first earthly priority. Otherwise he will feel last.

In their early years together, Solomon's bride apparently put his interests above her own. She was so looking forward to being with him that their lives intertwined enjoyably.

Putting your kids before your husband can not only cripple a marriage, it can eventually end it. Keep in mind your kids will one day be out of the house (hopefully!), but you've got your husband for life! Think about the dynamic of that for a moment. As the mother hen, your goal is that your baby birds eventually spread their wings, learn to fly, and leave you and your husband with an empty nest. But your goal when it comes to your husband is that he *never* leave. You launch your children into a life of their own, but you love your husband for life. Your goal as a parent is ultimately to get the kids OUT of the house; your goal as a wife is stay married to your husband. The best way to let him know that you are committed to him for a lifetime is to not put him "on hold" or make him stand in line behind the kids until they're out on their own.

Putting your kids before your husband can not only cripple a marriage, it can eventually end it.

Yet far too many wives do this. As a result, they often regret it later in their married life.

A Love Story Gone Wrong

One of the Bible's great love stories is recorded in Genesis 24. It's a story of an arranged marriage, but it's also a story of God sovereignly bringing two people together. It's a story of a couple's "love at first sight," of a growing love through the sorrows and struggles of life, and a deepening trust in God to faithfully work within their midst to fulfill His promises.

But what starts as one of the Bible's great love stories ends as a lesson in what NOT to do in marriage. It shows us that even the best starts can go sour if we, as wives, are not committed to putting our husbands first. Let me paraphrase and flesh out for you the story found in Genesis 24–27.

Isaac walked out to the fields to pray at sunset. It had been a long day, and there was much on his mind. The caravan would be returning any day now. And when he saw them approaching he would know whether or not his father's plan to find him a wife from among his relatives nearby would be successful.

God, is this the day? Will my father's servant return with a woman who is willing to leave everyone she knows to come here and be my wife? Lord, You know all things. You also know I'm 40 years old and You promised my father You would bring about a nation of people through his sole descendent—through me. God, it's been a long time waiting. Yet still I...

Before he'd finished praying he noticed the caravan of camels approaching. He squinted to see if coming back with them was a woman he would be able to call his own. He walked toward them, ready for the news, whatever it was.

Across the field, Rebekah must have seen him at the same time. She dismounted from her camel and asked, "Who is that man walking in the fields to meet us?" When she learned the man was the one she would marry, she took her veil and covered herself.

As Isaac approached, his father's servant told him the incredible story—that he had prayed that God would show him from among Abraham's relatives the woman who would be Isaac's wife by having her not only give him a drink of water but offer to water his ten camels as well. The servant told him that Rebekah, the virgin daughter of his cousin, had showed up before he even finished praying and gave him a drink and offered to water his ten camels too. The servant explained that Rebekah didn't hesitate to leave her family and travel to an unknown land to be Isaac's bride, even after her family tried to persuade her to delay her departure for another ten days.

Isaac was smitten by Rebekah's beauty, her respect, her mannerisms. The more he learned of her, the more he was moved by her courageous heart and the fact that she left home, by the word of his father's servant, to come marry a man she didn't even know. He would make sure she never regretted that decision.

Isaac took Rebekah's hand and led her into the tent occupied by his mother before she died. That evening he married her, and experienced for the first time since the loss of his mother a sense of comfort and hope for his future.

But their future didn't unfold the way they thought it would. Rebekah struggled for *years* with not being able to have a child. But Isaac didn't give up on his wife. He pleaded with the Lord to open her womb, and God allowed her to become pregnant not just with a son but with *twins.*

Sadly, after the birth of twin boys, their story went a different direction—down a path that divided the two of them, divided the kids, and left Rebekah alienated and alone in her household.

The Great Divide

Rebekah found a new love once she became a mom—the youngest twin, Jacob, a gentle, quiet boy whom she immediately favored. He liked to be in and around the tents with her so she chose him to be "Mama's boy" and help her with food preparation, cooking, and all the indoor chores. That didn't appear to bother Isaac because he was fonder of the older twin, Esau, a ruddy, sturdy young boy who loved the outdoors where the men worked. Isaac taught his firstborn to be a skilled hunter and a true outdoorsman who brought home the kind of kill Isaac loved to eat. Rebekah taught Jacob to be a skilled chef and cook that meat and feed the entire household. Anyone looking on might have thought these parents had figured out how to manage the household quite efficiently, dividing up the talents of the twins and working together like a well-oiled machine. But we see something glaringly evident in that story. Once the children arrived, there was no more "us" when it came to Isaac and Rebekah. Their "us" was replaced by the existence of *two* teams—and each parent was on a different one.

When the boys got older, Jacob (whose name literally means "deceiver") tricked his hardworking and nearly starving brother into selling his birthright for a pot of stew. And it only got worse from there. I wonder if the sense of competition between those boys extended to their parents. All we know is something went terribly wrong. The distance between Isaac and Rebekah that started when their twins were born widened into a huge gap by the time Isaac was old. He wished to place his blessing on his oldest son, Esau, and his once-beloved wife schemed with Jacob to trick her nearly blind husband into giving the birthright and blessing to Jacob instead.

If Isaac had gone to his grave unaware of what his wife had done to deceive him, we might have hope that they departed this earth as a couple still in love. But Scripture says he "trembled violently" and "wept aloud" when it occurred to him he had been tricked into blessing the wrong son (Genesis 27:33,38)! Shortly after that, Esau vowed to kill his brother for tricking him out of his blessing and Rebekah helped Jacob leave so his life would be spared. Her words were, "Why should I lose both of you in one day?" (verse 45). She had to have known her older son would resent her for what she did to help his brother cheat him out of his birthright. And after all of that went down, Rebekah had the nerve to lie again to her husband in order to get Jacob away from his brother who now hated him. So that Isaac would bless Jacob and send him away to find a wife, Rebekah told him, "I'm disgusted with living because of these Hittite women. If Jacob takes a wife from among the women of this land...my life will not be worth living."

Really, Rebekah? Your life became all about Jacob to the point that it wouldn't be worth living anymore if he didn't marry well? What about your husband's life now that his wife has deceived him? What about his misery with the mistake (and the deceit of his wife and son) that he has to now live with?

I imagine when the boys left home, there remained a cold tension between Isaac and Rebekah. She had invested her life in planning Jacob's future, to the point that she betrayed her husband and their intimacy. The result? She was left at home without either of her children and with a husband who knew she had tricked him.

Rebekah traded her husband's favor for her younger son's future. And in the end she lost all three of them. (Jacob moved far away so Esau wouldn't find him and kill him. Esau left to find a wife too. And Isaac was distraught with the knowledge that his wife had become as conniving as his youngest son.)

One commentator wrote, "Even if her motive was pure (in giving her son the birthright that God said he would one day have—Genesis 25:23) [Rebekah's] action was wrong. She paid a bitter price in living out her final years in separation from the son whose presence she desired, in alienation from the son who would ever remember his mother's deception toward him, and in broken fellowship from a husband who had loved her devotedly."[1]

It's so sad to me that Isaac and Rebekah aren't remembered today for being a loving couple, but for being a lesson in what *not* to do when it comes to putting kids and personal ambition above your marriage.

I know you don't want to experience what Rebekah did when you and your husband reach your golden years. In fact, you want those years to be "golden," not "guilt-ridden," so don't make your husband compete with something or someone else.

Show Him He's Priority

In *When a Woman Inspires Her Husband*, I wrote about how very important it is to a man to be affirmed, admired, and respected. It all boils down to becoming his cheerleader who will stand by him through thick and thin—through child rearing and career climbing and whatever else may come your way. As you show him he's priority, you'll earn his trust, ignite his passion, and increase his desire for communication.

Here are some practical ways to make sure your actions show him he's first in everything you do.

Create Quality Moments for the Two of You

Emily, a 29-year-old teacher, has been married to George for seven years. Now that they have two young children, she is seeing how very easy it is to neglect him if she's not careful.

"My love language is quality time," Emily said. "This is hard to get in our marriage these days since we have a newborn and a two-year-old. We are extremely busy with our kids and rarely even get moments to ourselves. When we do get a moment, we tend to want to be alone (I like to read; George likes to play videogames on the computer). These alone moments are important, yet it can lead to us becoming distant toward each other. So I often try to find ways for us to have 'quality time' as a couple so we don't become distant. We have no problem sending the kids to Grandma's house for the night so we can have a date night and focus on each other. For example, we recently celebrated our seven-year anniversary and our newborn was only six weeks old. You better believe we still went out for the weekend and left the kids with Grandma so that we could prioritize our marriage. The kids survived, and we had uninterrupted, amazing conversations all weekend long!"

Consider His Needs Too

Emily said she knows in her head that putting her marriage first is important, but because selfishness comes natural to everyone, it's easy to forget and think of only her need for space and alone time, rather than her husband's too. So she's been trying to reverse that.

"When I've had a long, difficult day with the kids and am so glad to hear that George is home, my first instinct is to throw the kids at him and run out the door so I can be alone. But sometimes I think about him first and remember that he, too, has had a long, hard day at work and probably would like a shower since he is covered in sawdust, dirt, and fiberglass. So instead of running from the house, I tell him to take his shower and decompress, and I get to hang with the crying children a little bit longer."

Commit to Weekly Time Together

My cousin Lisa, 34, said she and her husband of seven years resurrected date nights once they realized how very important it was for them to focus on each other amidst the distraction of several children between the two of them!

"Whether it's weekly or once a month, we purposely set aside a night to go out just the two of us. The drive is usually spent getting each other caught up on anything one of our kids has going on. When we get to our date location (beach, restaurant, theater) we switch into 'us' mode. We don't talk about work or the kids. I ask him about vacations he wants to go on, races he wants to run, the truck or motorcycle he's working on, whatever he's interested in."

Rally Around Him

When you talk up your husband in front of your children and others, it not only presents the two of you as a united front, but it says to him, "I'm on your team" and "I support you." Nothing cements your bond stronger than when others—including the kids—know you two are inseparable.

Nothing cements your bond stronger than when others—including the kids—know you two are inseparable.

Prepare Your Heart for Him

My friend Allison is a longtime women's ministries director who has been happily married to Guy for more than 30 years. She kept her husband a priority while the kids were younger and still does today by planning for their time together at the end of the day. "Near the end of each work day, one of us will call the other to give a heads-up on how the day has gone—almost to prepare our hearts and minds for what our evening time together will be like. This was a huge blessing when I was staying home while the kids were little. Guy would check in with me to see if I needed anything so he could pick it up on the way home. And I could prepare my mind and heart to be a wife to him again, and not just a mom to the kids. It really helped me get my head wrapped around all that he had faced at work and helped improve the outlook of the day when we got back together at night."

Put Him Above Your Parents

Many husbands resent coming second to their wife's parents. Your husband wants and needs to know you will defer to him even over your own dad. That might be tough if you have a close relationship with your father and you feel the tug to still be daddy's girl. But you are your husband's wife first. Honor him by letting him know his opinions and preferences weigh the most in your heart.

Put Him Above Your Ministry

I know many women who give so much time to their church or ministry that they fail to realize their first ministry is to their husband. Jennifer has been married for decades to a man who is an unbeliever. Yet they have a great marriage, and it's because Jennifer goes by the motto "Feed him first." Jennifer is determined to honor God by honoring her husband, and he doesn't resent her being involved in various ministries and activities at church because she makes sure she tends to him first before going out the door. When she takes snacks or a dessert to a women's function or is planning to be gone for a weekend, she leaves him with the same snacks or desserts, or a refrigerator full of meals for the weekend so he never has the chance to wonder if he is less important to her than her faith and friends.

PRAYING IT THROUGH

You can experience more with your husband when you let him know he is number one on your priority list, just below God. Here's a prayer to that effect:

> *God, You knew when You brought me into my husband's life what our lives would look like today. You knew the schedules, the distractions, the challenges. And yet You are still here, waiting to help me as I call upon You. Help me, dear Lord, to*

prioritize my husband above everyone else. May he be second in my life next to You only. Give me discernment to see the times he might be waiting in line or feeling he's been put "on hold." And give me grace to rectify that and return him to a place of honor that pleases You. In Jesus' name, amen.

YOUR FOCUS FOR THE WEEK

What are three tangible ways you can let your husband know he's the first priority in your life, second only to God? Pick a few from this chapter or write some of your own in the space below. Commit to them this week as a nonverbal way of saying, "You mean more to me than anyone or anything else." (And *verbally* saying that, by the way, won't hurt either.)

1.

2.

3.

4

Let It Go

Practicing Acceptance, Not Accusation

As far as the east is from the west, so far has he removed our transgressions from us.

Psalm 103:12

Would you classify yourself as a tosser or a keeper?

Hugh and I had this conversation while we were still dating. He and I both descended from *keepers*—people who spent a lifetime amassing stuff and rarely got rid of anything. Keepers are sometimes intense collectors—they keep piles of old magazines, clothes they haven't worn in years, tools, extra utensils, jewelry, knickknacks, and pieces of this and that because "you never know when you might need them."

Because we each grew up around keepers, we were determined once we got married to be *tossers.* We would collect only adventures, experiences, and memories that added to the value of our lives, not stuff that would take up space. And we vowed to toss the unnecessary, the junk, the *things* that many couples let amass over the years that are worth very little.

Through the years, Hugh and I have strayed a bit from that goal we made when we married. I ended up collecting Cinderella dolls and figurines (mostly because Hugh—and family members—kept giving them to me!), and Hugh collected *Star Trek* memorabilia (but hey, he'll make a fortune from it on eBay one day, right?). Yet the real conversation we should have had before we married was whether we were tossers or keepers when it came to our hurts and offenses.

Someone who can forgive is a tosser. One who can't let it go is a keeper.

Which One Are You?

Are you a tosser or a keeper when it comes to offenses in your marriage? Take the test for yourself by circling "yes" after the statements that describe you and "no" to the statements that don't.

I tend to get irritated by something my husband continually does.	Yes/No
My husband and I continue to argue about the same issues.	Yes/No
I tend to generalize about my husband with statements like, "He never stops for directions" or "He's always late" or "He's a lousy tipper at restaurants" after a couple of incidents.	Yes/No
I've been known to bring up an issue after we've already resolved it.	Yes/No
I sometimes bring up ways that he's hurt me in the past when we are discussing a different issue.	Yes/No
My mind often returns to past pain or offenses.	Yes/No
I can get "triggered" by words or phrases and respond negatively, causing my husband to look at me and wonder what it was he said.	Yes/No

Now add up your "yes" answers.

If you have 5–7 "yes" answers, thank you for your honesty. This chapter is definitely for you. (And I don't feel like I'm such a loser now, since those questions pretty much described me at one time too.) If you have 2–4 "yes" statements, this chapter is still for you. If you have 0–1 "yes" answers, you should be writing this book. I'm serious. You are the Queen of Letting It Go. But please stick with me so you can learn some helpful hints for your married girlfriends who are most likely "keepers" and will need these tips.*

Now that you know the difference between a tosser and a keeper when it comes to personal offenses, read on to see what damage can come to a keeper and how to reverse the habit.

Keeping Score

I sat for coffee with Beth and listened to the words I never thought I'd hear.

She was telling me why she'd left her husband after more than 20 years.

"He's changed a lot over the past five years," she said. "He's not the same man I married. I wonder now if I was *ever* loved."

Although my heart went out to her for the pain she was experiencing, it certainly wasn't the first time I'd heard a woman cite that reason for leaving her marriage. I just never expected to hear it from Beth. She and her husband had so much going for them. Their problems sounded like the ones every couple experiences. I was certain their marriage was workable.

She assured me she wasn't bitter, just resolved that it was time to walk away. I asked Beth if she thought *she* had changed at all in the past five years, since all of us grow and change to some degree. I wondered, too, what she had let accumulate to get to the point where she wanted out. Sadly, my friend was unable to let some things go.

Erasing the Score

Maybe your complaint is not that your husband has changed. Maybe *you* have. And that is causing problems.

My friend Lisa and her husband were both unbelievers when they

---

* I don't even mind if you claim these "helpful hints" came from *you*.

married. Two years into their marriage, she began following Christ and her lifestyle changed. Her husband wanted the "party hearty" girl back, but that wasn't who she was anymore. They've been together more than 32 years now, and although Lisa's husband is now a believer, she credits forgiveness and the ability to "let it go" as the key to their strength as a couple today.

"My husband has many a regret due to his addictions," Lisa said. "Forgiveness has got to be the number one ingredient to us being together today. He lives under such condemnation from the devil the last thing he needs is me reminding him of the past or bringing up his present struggles."

Lisa has learned not to keep score and to erase offenses. Sometimes on a daily basis she has to leave the past in the past and let it go. And because of that she is experiencing so much more with her husband today.

Love Is Blind

I'm sure you've often heard the phrase "Love is blind." We say it about couples who are first starting to date or about newlyweds. We even give it a negative connotation when we say things like, "She has no idea what she's getting herself into. But...love is blind."

Then when we get to the point where we can really see our husbands' faults we believe we've attained a certain level of maturity.

I believe Solomon's new bride, whom we looked at in chapters 2 and 3, was "blind" too. Blind to her husband's faults. Or maybe as a woman in love, she *chose* to overlook them. The more I think about it, the more I realize today that it wouldn't hurt for you and me to be "blind" to the faults of our husbands. Just as "love is blind" when a woman in love doesn't see the things that would otherwise annoy her, love must CHOOSE to be blind when it comes to the things about your husband and mine that will never change. Just as our eyes dim with age, what if we became more blind with age to our husbands' faults?

It wouldn't hurt to be blind to the faults of our husbands.

Admit it, you want your husband to see only the best in you. You would love for his eyes to become less critical and more "soft focused" on your body parts and imperfect personality parts as he ages. But can you do the same for him? You can learn to become blind to your husband's faults if you can learn to let some things go.

Now, I'm not talking about putting up with behavior that is unhealthy. Nor am I talking about becoming a doormat. I'm talking about realizing you are a sinner by nature and so is your husband (Romans 3:23), and that means the two of you together are a mess that God is willing to redeem. I'm talking about extending grace and showing patience toward one another. I'm talking about learning to let it go.

When you and I refuse to let something go in our marriage, we are choosing *not* to forgive. We might not see it that way. But that's what it is. When we hold on to something, cling to it, bury it deep inside, and even dredge it up now and then to remind ourselves—and our husbands—how much they have hurt us, we are refusing to forgive. We are harboring resentment in our hearts. We are allowing our hearts to harden.

When you and I refuse to let something go in our marriage, we are choosing not *to forgive.*

Understanding Your Pain—and His

Why is it sometimes so difficult to let things go?

Robin Reinke, a licensed marriage and family therapist who sees women and couples in her practice every day, says we often react the way we do out of our pain. Certain words or situations will trigger pain in us and we end up reacting defensively.

"We sometimes interpret our husbands' words or actions from a deep place of pain and then what may have just been considered a "misdemeanor" in our minds becomes a felony. That causes us to store in our hearts certain offenses that aren't really from them at all. It's often a resurfacing wound that we have to deal with.

"I realize now that when couples complain that their spouse is changing, it usually means that their hearts have closed to the marriage because of some minor violation of trust or hurt that has never been addressed," Robin says. It's also possible that "either he's being the same guy and you've become critical or he's living out of his pain cycle."

Every one of us receives minor violations, offenses, and hurts that rub us the wrong way. Sometimes we choose not to talk about them. Or we try to talk it out, but there isn't healthy conflict resolution. We then hold on to it or bury it. Either way we don't let it go and our hearts gradually harden. When our hearts harden, we become critical and hopeless, and this is when people proclaim "I'm done!"

Scripture warns us in Proverbs 4:23 to guard our hearts so they don't harden:

> Above all else, guard your heart,
> for everything you do flows from it.

I believe we are told in this verse not only to guard what we let into our hearts but to guard our hearts themselves from hardening so they don't become a harbor for our hurts, resentments, and eventually bitterness.

In the New American Standard Bible, Proverbs 4:23 reads like this:

> Watch over your heart with all diligence,
> For from it flow the springs of life.

I find it interesting in Song 4:15 that Solomon told his young bride:

> You are a garden fountain,
> a well of flowing water
> streaming down from Lebanon.

This makes me believe a woman with a hardened heart is one whose heart is dammed up, preventing the flow of what would normally spring from it—kindness, forgiveness, laughter, generosity. Solomon felt refreshed by his bride, who probably let laughter and joy flow readily from her heart. He saw her as a garden fountain, a well of *flowing* water that was streaming. In short, her love—and her whole demeanor—was refreshing to him.

You can be a flowing, bubbling spring in your husband's life, not a stagnant swamp, when you keep your heart softened, flexible, forgiving. Instead of holding on to hurts and harboring them in your heart, learn how to freely let them go. Be a tosser, not a keeper, when it comes to offenses.

Be a tosser, not a keeper, when it comes to offenses.

Robin's definition of how one closes off their heart to their marriage describes you and me anytime we choose to hold on to little hurts and offenses. And I believe it explains nearly every marriage I've seen struggle. It explains nearly every marriage I've seen crumble. And it explains to me why so many wives wish they could experience so much more with their husbands but don't.

My "Aha" Moment

I think I finally learned how to truly forgive, let it go, and move on when I took the time to learn about who my husband is, wounds and all. This didn't come from several hours of communication. He's an introvert, and expressing his feelings verbally has never and still doesn't come easily to him. It came from reading a couple of books. One was about his introverted personality.* The other book was about how men with certain personalities process wounds.† These books helped me understand why my husband responds the way he does to conflict (or perceived conflict) and to accusation (or perceived accusation). It gave me great insight as to why my husband is the way he is at times, why he

---

* It was a book called *Quiet: The Power of Introverts in a World That Can't Stop Talking.* Talk about gaining a better understanding of the sometimes-painful world my husband lives in when I won't stop talking!

† The other book was called *The Silent Cry of Christian Women: Breaking Passive Aggressive Cycles* by Dee Brown.

is incapable of responding to certain questions, and why he sometimes goes silent. As I read those books I remembered certain conversations he and I had had in the past, and situations he had told me about concerning his upbringing, how he was disciplined, what he feared, how he wasn't allowed to respond when being lectured, how he felt when he was being punished. I guess you could say reading about his personality was eye-opening and reading about past wounds that have shaped him was heartbreaking.

After reading those books I had a long talk with my husband about what I learned, and I saw in his eyes both pain at having to admit that those wounds were real and relief that finally someone understood him—and was helping him understand more of himself as well.

I think coming face-to-face with his brokenness (and mine) helped me see him through God's eyes. He isn't trying to anger me. He isn't trying to wound me when he says something defensive or rude from my perspective. He isn't ignoring me when he finds himself unable to respond to something I've said. He is simply processing through the filter of past wounds.

In seeking to understand Hugh and the wounds in his past, I also learned a little more about my own wounds and why I respond to Hugh the way I do. I grew up in an environment where there was no emotional filter. We expressed *everything*—physical pain, emotional pain, anger, embarrassment, shame, delight, you name it!—and we expressed it loudly, emotionally, dramatically. I also grew up with an alcoholic father who was a closet drinker, so I learned to be suspicious of others if I didn't get all the details and if those details didn't add up right in my mind. Instead of giving someone the benefit of the doubt, I had them tried and convicted in my mind.

When I realized the baggage I was carrying and how that stacked up next to the baggage Hugh was carrying, it began to make sense to me why we interact with each other the way we do at times. It made sense to me why I aggressively launch an attack when I sense conflict and why my husband retreats in the opposite direction. It also made me so much more appreciative of the grace God extends to the broken, His ability to keep us together in spite of our dysfunction, and

His Holy Spirit's transforming power to redeem us into people who are whole and healed.

You and I can experience so much more with our husbands—more trust, more passion, more understanding, and more communication—when we learn what is going on in their hearts and minds and what pain in their past triggers certain actions and reactions, and then extend grace as we realize "my husband is just as broken as I am."

Marriage Is Messy

Marriage is *so messy.* It's messy because people are messy. Because you and I—and our husbands—are broken messes who are trying to make sense of life and trying to live together under one roof and somewhere in all of that find a happily ever after.

The Bible says, "For all have sinned and fall short of the glory of God" (Romans 3:23). Not only have we sinned and piled up mistakes from our past, but we sometimes continue to operate in a wounded fashion. And our husbands do the same.

And yet it is possible to get off that merry-go-round.* You and I can give up the "accusation dance" by introducing the "grace maneuver." It goes like this:

You and I can give up the "accusation dance" by introducing the "grace maneuver."

I am broken. I have been hurt in the past just like every other human being on this earth, and certain situations trigger less than flattering actions and reactions from me. I regret these responses and ask God to, once again, heal me of those wounds so I don't experience flare-ups at my husband. Then, instead of shining the flashlight on what my husband is doing wrong, or how he's failing to meet my expectations,

* Definition of the "McMenamin Merry-go-round": I accuse, then he accuses, then I defend, and he counter-defends, so I accuse some more as his eyes glaze over…are you dizzy yet?

or why he is acting downright caveman at times, I'm going to extend grace because I realize he is broken too. And the times that *he* acts less than flattering are the times he needs my grace and kindness the most. I will let this incident (or remark) go. And I will quietly thank God that just as I have chosen to overlook my husband's offense, God has overlooked ten million of my own.

Just as I have chosen to overlook my husband's offense, God has overlooked ten million of my own.

Now, if it sounds like I'm being super dramatic or even super hard on you and me it's because we tend to look down on our husbands every time they disappoint us. Every time they don't live up to our expectations. Every time they leave that darned toilet seat up, or don't come home at the time they said they would, or take the long way to get somewhere, or refuse to ask for directions or help. We can let our hearts get poked each time they do something that ruffles our feathers, rubs us the wrong way, or makes us feel devalued. Yet those are the times we need to extend grace to them as God has extended it to us. Those are the times our husbands most need our understanding, patience, and forgiveness.

Moving Forward

You can become a woman of understanding, patience, and forgiveness—a woman who is a spring of life to your husband—when you practice some of these forward-moving steps that will help you let go of offenses:

Identify what triggers pain in your life. Robin said, "We get triggered and then we believe the lie—for example, that we're not valued or we're alone or we're not appreciated or respected. The first step is recognition. We have to recognize and identify what is causing our pain. And most of the time your spouse is not the root of the problem. The problem is often connected to past wounds or present pain in your own life." What triggers *your* pain? Is it the fear of being rejected? The fear of abandonment? The feeling that you're being criticized or devalued? Do you get triggered by the idea that you are suffering by comparison or not measuring up to someone's expectations? Identify your fear and your pain. Name it. And then move on to the next step. (Reinke recommends the book, *5 Days to a New Marriage* by Dr. Terry Hargrave and Dr. Shawn Stoever, which will help you identify your pain-peace cycle and learn the four steps to healthy conflict resolution and connection.)

Surrender your pain to the only One who can heal it. "Jesus is our only safety," said Robin. When we expect someone else to give us value or security or significance or heal our pain they will fail every time. We can only find that deep sense of security and fulfillment from the Maker of our soul. Let Him heal those *deep wounds in your heart.*[1]

Know your true identity so you can combat the lies. As you become aware of Whose you are—a child of the living God—and your identity in that deepens, you have a greater capacity to filter offenses and become more emotionally tuned in, understanding, and accepting of your husband. It is then that you can realize you may have acted poorly and the problem isn't really with him.

Practice grace and forgiveness. To show our husbands grace and forgiveness, we need to let go of our pride and our insistence on being right and humble ourselves. We need to forgive as God has forgiven us.

Leave the past where it belongs. Allison said forgiveness and being able to "bury the hatchet" is one of the reasons she and her husband have stayed strong together for more than 30 years. "Take one day at a time and leave the past behind you," she said. "Garth Brooks used to sing a country song about a couple who would bury the hatchet but leave the handle sticking out, presumably to pull it up out of the ground each time and start fighting again. Leave the past in the past, and if an issue has been resolved, leave it out of new discussions."

God's Model to Us

The refusal to forgive not only splits marriages but families, parent-child relationships, friendships, and even churches. Yet God modeled a forgiveness and a "let it go" mentality when it comes to His relationship with us:

> As far as the east is from the west, so far has He removed our transgressions from us (Psalm 103:12 NKJV).

Furthermore, Micah 7:19 says:

> You will again have compassion on us;
> you will tread our sins underfoot
> and hurl all our iniquities into the depths of the sea.

When something is "as far as the east is from the west"—from infinity to infinity—it cannot be pulled back together again. Neither can something that God has buried in the depths of the sea be dredged back up again. When we let something go—whether it merely bothered us or nearly destroyed us—we are showing forgiveness to our husbands and showing God we understand the extent to which *He* forgave us. God hurled our offenses far from us and from Him. He expects us to do the same when it comes to forgiving others.

Practice acceptance, not accusation. Freely forgive. You will experience more with your husband—and perhaps even recapture his heart—when you become a woman who can let it go.

PRAYING IT THROUGH

In my book *When a Woman Overcomes Life's Hurts*, I offer a prayer that I encourage women to say in their hearts or even aloud to release offenses that could otherwise build up and start hardening in their hearts and destroying their relationships. The beauty of this prayer is that it also releases the one saying it so she isn't encumbered anymore with something she previously couldn't let go.

I believe this prayer is healing when said in relation to our husbands as well. Fill in the blanks in this prayer with your husband's name and what it was that he did that you are tempted to hold on to every time something starts sticking in your mind or heart as an offense. Then say this prayer in your heart or aloud, as a way of releasing it to God:

> *Lord, I choose to forgive ______________________________*
> *for____,*
> *even though it made me feel __________________________.*
> *I surrender these feelings to You and ask that You remove my expectation that my husband can and will repair those wounds that only You can heal. Help me see him through Your eyes and readily extend grace to him as You have extended it to me. Finally, help me rely on You alone to fill the broken places in my heart. In Jesus' name, amen.*

Think of the many things that can stack up in a marriage. Now, what if you took each one through the grid of that prayer and, as you did, you let it go? There would be nothing left to hang on to that could drive a wedge between the two of you. And you will be giving your husband—and yourself—the gift of freedom that comes through forgiveness.

YOUR FOCUS FOR THE WEEK

Write or print out the prayer above and post it in a place where you can see it (on your desk, your refrigerator door, your car dashboard, your bedroom mirror, or make it your computer or cell phone screen saver!). Note how many times you pray it this week so you can be aware of how easily offenses start stacking up, and how easily you can release them to God and practice the daily discipline of letting it go.

5

Switch It Up

Incorporating New Habits at Home

She watches over the affairs of her household.

PROVERBS 31:27

A sign over the front door of a women's spa read, "Leave your baggage at the door. This is a place of peace and rest."

How my marriage and yours would be different if that sign hung over our own front doors, reminding us of the importance of peace on the other side of the door. And how our marriages would be different if we really treated our spouse as a guest who was coming to our home to seek peace and rest.

Admit it, you and I are often at our best when we have guests visiting. We want to make a good impression so others will feel at home. The Bible instructs us to practice hospitality toward one another. But what if we were to practice the hospitality outlined in 1 Peter 4:8-9 toward our husbands just as we would toward guests in our home?

First Peter 4:8-9 says, "Above all, love each other deeply, because love covers over a multitude of sins. Offer hospitality to one another without grumbling."

You know what I'm talking about. There are certain things we do to make our guests feel at home:

- We aim to make them feel comfortable.

- We speak kindly and politely.
- We are on our best behavior.
- We make sure the house is clean.
- We serve them (Can I get you something to drink?) and we are glad to feed them.
- We are attentive when they talk and we tend to their needs.

There are also certain things we just wouldn't do in the presence of our guests:

- Raise our voices.
- Respond rudely.
- Fail to acknowledge when they come through the door.
- Tell them, "Get it yourself."
- Make a fuss when they don't pick up after themselves.

You can probably guess where I'm going with this. You watch what you say and do in the presence of others, but what if you were to do the same thing in the presence of your husband? What if you were to treat him like a guest each time he came through the door?

I got to thinking about how appropriate that sign would be over my own front door as a reminder of how to enter my home and how to treat my husband when he enters as well. Admittedly, my husband and I have unintentionally brought baggage through our front door over the years—baggage that we've learned can reside in the walls of our home and eventually *build* walls between the two of us.

After nearly 30 years of marriage—including 20 years of my husband and me counseling other couples on how to maintain a closer connection—I'm convinced that it's the simple, unintentional things that eventually become *huge*, offensive things that slowly undermine the security and health of a marriage. Like the one dropped stitch that will eventually cause an entire sweater to unravel, one critical word, one careless act, or one forgotten gesture can lead to resentment that eventually unravels the foundation of your relationship.[1] Likewise, when baggage from wounds and present irritations goes unchecked, it can wreak reckless words, unintended silence, or hurtful behavior we aren't even aware of. But those behaviors can be reversed.

Cleaning House

If you've brought baggage into your home through the years—from something in your past or just day-to-day frustrations in your present—you can still learn to check it at the door and improve the overall atmosphere of your home so it resembles a place of peace and rest. And if you are starting your journey with your husband and it's too soon for the baggage, it's not too soon to start making sure you don't ever let it begin to make its way through your front or back door.

First Corinthians 13:5 tells us that love, among other things, "does not dishonor others, it is not self-seeking, it is not easily angered, it keeps no record of wrongs." Although we are not to keep record of our spouse's wrongs, if we are aware of our *own* relational wrongs, we can start reversing those unintentional actions and rebuild the relationship with simple acts of love.

That's what my husband and I learned to do. We switched it up. We started doing things the other didn't expect…in a good way. And you can too. Here are some new habits to practice every day that will turn your hearts toward each other and not only increase your husband's desire to be with you at home, but they should increase your desire to be with him as well. I like to think of these as "Seven Ways to Remove the Baggage and Rebuild Love."

We started doing things the other didn't expect…in a good way.

Reexamine Your Greetings and Good-byes

How do you greet someone you love whom you haven't seen in a while? And how do you tell them good-bye if you know it will be awhile before you reunite? Even if you see your spouse every day, and have for years, your greetings—and good-byes—are still important. Take note of how you greet each other when you or your spouse enters the front door. And how do you respond when you or your spouse leaves the house? How you greet each other in the morning as you wake and how you sign off at night before you sleep are important too. When you and I are careful about our entrances and exits—and our spouse's—we can ensure a more loving atmosphere in our homes.

When you and I are careful about our entrances and exits—and our spouse's—we can ensure a more loving atmosphere in our homes.

Resolve to Be a Mystery

How we greet and treat him in our home is not the only area in which we may need to switch it up. Try being a different woman when he walks through the door, a quieter woman, a woman with a secret, a *mysterious* woman.

In Song 4:12 Solomon sang this about his new bride: "You are a garden locked up, my sister, my bride; you are a spring enclosed, a sealed fountain."

Now, scholars say that implies she is a virgin. But I would like to think that is a statement about the unexplored territory of her mind, heart, and emotions that he would like to explore. Does your husband know what makes you tick? Make him think about it. The only way we will become intriguing to our husbands is if we don't put it all out there so that he has no more guesswork. Try smiling coyly when he asks how your day went, and don't be so quick to answer. Reach out and touch his face lovingly when he is sure you were going to correct him or give him a task. Switch it up. Don't be predictable.

The only way we will become intriguing to our husbands is if we don't put it all out there so that he has no more guesswork.

Queen Esther's story in the Bible is a great example of this. She piqued the interest of her husband, the king, by inviting him to dinner on three consecutive nights, telling him the first two times to come back the next night before she would give him her request. By the time she presented her request on the third night, the king was eager to fulfill it immediately. She had piqued his interest, built his curiosity, and won over his heart.

Release Your Expectations

We have so many expectations of our husbands, and whether we verbalize them or not, they know when they've disappointed us. Our expectations put undue pressure on our husbands and often set them up for failure. Practice the Bible's definition of love that "bears all things, believes all things, hopes all things, endures all things" (1 Corinthians 13:7 NASB) by realizing only God—and not your husband—can meet your emotional needs. Encourage your man with the words, "I love and accept you for who you are, not who I've been trying to make you become."

Our expectations put undue pressure on our husbands and often set them up for failure.

One of our biggest expectations is that our husbands are always going to be a certain way or that we're going to be able to change them into the men we'd prefer they be.

Debbie, a radio host and author who has been married 15 years, said, "My husband has changed in some ways that I'm not too thrilled about. I've had to let go of the fantasy that my husband will always be a certain way, and I've learned that it's best for me to remain focused on his good qualities instead of dwelling on the changes I don't like."

Request His List

Several years ago I left on a business trip while feeling a little wounded. I indicated to Hugh (through a phone call from the airport) that I wished he had been a little more affectionate to me before I left. So when I returned home from the trip I thought there might be flowers, a gift, an invitation to dinner, *something* to show a little extra effort on his part. There was none of that. Instead, Hugh handed me a plain white envelope. In it were two sheets of paper. One had on it the title "What I Need Most from You" and the other was titled "Foods I Like to Eat." (I'm not kidding. And I know what you're thinking already.)

On the sheet entitled "Foods I Like to Eat" Hugh wrote down the names of several dishes I had made through the years that he really liked. I believe that was his way of telling me he wanted me to start cooking them again. (I'm glad he emphasized the positive, rather than listing the meals I had cooked that he didn't like. I'll be the first to admit that probably would've been a much longer list!) The other page consisted of the top three things he needed from me intimately. That list included three words that we then had a conversation unpacking. His list said:

1. Visibility
2. Spontaneity
3. Creativity

Without giving you the intimate details of what Hugh and I talked about, I did learn, through the years, that sharing these three things with many other wives actually helped their sex life too. When they began to offer this "Top 3" to their husbands, they began to realize, too, that these three elements were not just unique to my husband. Men are men. They are wired visually. They like to be spontaneous. And they like to switch it up. Ask your husband what his "Top 3" preferences are when it comes to sexual intimacy. Does he, too, want visibility, spontaneity, and creativity? Maybe he is a guy who simply wants you to be more verbal when it comes to telling him what you prefer sexually. Ask him. And be willing to switch it up.

Men are men. They are wired visually. They like to be spontaneous. And they like to switch it up.

Release Your Inhibitions

Allison, whom I introduced to you in chapter 3, is forthright in letting wives know about the importance of being sexually uninhibited with their husbands.

"Most men are very visual, and although it may be harder for some wives to embrace a positive image about their body, be *regularly* generous and demonstrative in your physical love for your husband," she said. "Be brave and committed to sharing your body freely with him within your marriage—even if or when it feels awkward. This may even include talking more during your intimate times, or talking about what gives each of you pleasure or enjoyment. And remember, confidence is the best aphrodisiac."

Like Allison, my friend Lisa, whom I referred to in chapter 3, is also a longtime women's ministry director,* and she, too, is candid about what is necessary to keep passion in marriage.

"As women, we are not always comfortable in our bodies. Finding creative ways to be sexy without having to dance on a pole is tricky," Lisa said while blushing.†

---

* Okay, is there a connection between women's ministry directors and wives who are sexually uninhibited? Maybe it's just that women who tend to be leaders (as in leading a ministry to other women) are confident enough to "lead" when it comes to sexual intimacy too. So much for the "Christian women are prudes" stereotype!

† Now, let me be clear: Just because Lisa is not comfortable pole-dancing is not to suggest that it's wrong for you to give it a try in the confines of your home, for your husband's eyes only. If it sounds intriguing to you and you believe your husband would dig it, go for it.

"So I ordered a gypsy scarf online—black, sheer with gold jingly things and prayed, *Lord Jesus, help me be free to be what my husband needs me to be!* It took a lot of courage and moving through the awkwardness. The point was to sway with music behind the scarf. I think only I felt the awkwardness because he was absolutely delighted that I would think of him before my own comfort. Also, when I took the time once to watch a YouTube video on how to give a good massage, he was flattered—and a bit taken back—that I even gave it the effort." Are there some areas in which you need to lose your inhibitions in order to "switch it up"? I have a feeling your husband will *love* it.

Remember to Touch

When your life is full with so many things it's easy to forget what you used to do with your hands. You most likely used to touch your husband a lot more than you do now. Over the years Hugh and I have found that touch is more important than we realized. Reach out with a tender touch before getting out of bed. Kiss and hug each other every morning before one of you leaves the house. Reach across the table or the couch to hold your spouse's hand, even if only for a few moments. Reach over to rub his shoulder if he's disgruntled, distant, or could just use a backrub. Research shows that married couples who practice this simple daily discipline of affectionate touch are much healthier than those that don't.

When your life is full with so many things it's easy to forget what you used to do with your hands.

Remove the Zig-Zag

I learned in geometry that the shortest distance between two points is a straight line. Yet how we zig-zag in our relationships! Husbands and wives all start out heading in the same direction because we can't imagine being apart. But then we begin to proceed in different directions, even when living under the same roof. Different schedules, different interests, and different priorities eventually lead to different destinations and eventually indifference. To remove the zig-zag, begin asking your husband daily, "How can I pray for you?" or "Tell me one thing I can do for you today to make your day easier." And if the pressures of life have made you—or your spouse—a bit distant lately, offer verbal affirmation that you are still on your husband's team and your heart is still going in his direction.

WORKING IT THROUGH

How can you change it up at home? Start dressing differently (or better) than you do now. If you're the talker, do less talking so he will begin to wonder why you're quiet. If you're one to do what he expects, then take him by surprise, but in a good way.

Switch it up. Keep him guessing. Make him feel that you are just as committed to your marriage today as you were the day you two wed. And make that sign that hung outside the health spa if you need to—or write it on a Post-it note and stick it in your car so you can see it before you head into your house.

You will experience more with your husband when you become a woman who can switch it up and keep him guessing.

YOUR FOCUS FOR THE WEEK

Each day this week practice one of the seven ways you can switch it up. Record below any observable responses from your husband so you will remember which ones resonate the most with him.

Day of the week: ______________________________
—Reexamine your greetings and good-byes

His response:

Day of the week: ________________________
—Resolve to be a mystery

His response:

Day of the week: ________________________
—Release your expectations

His response:

Day of the week: ________________________
—Request his list

His response:

Day of the week: ________________________
—Release your inhibitions

His response:

Day of the week: ______________________

—Remember to touch

His response:

Day of the week: ______________________

— Remove the zig-zag

His response:

6

Let Him Breathe

Giving Up the Smothering, Mothering, and Hovering

For your husband is your Maker,
Whose name is the LORD of hosts.

ISAIAH 54:5 NASB

Barbara believed she was finally in that place where nothing could shake her.

As a 49-year-old, four-year-celibate woman, she had convinced herself she was standing firm. She was bulletproof. She'd been wounded through a previous marriage and relationships, but now she'd found Jesus as her Bridegroom. She realized she didn't *need* another man in her life anymore. And that realization was freeing.

Barbara recalled one night in particular when she felt confident she could be single the rest of her life as long as she had Jesus.

"One night as I lay in my big king-sized bed surrounded by my three grandkids—one sweet little girl and two handsome boys (all born within three years)—I smiled and thought to myself, *Lord, if these grandsons are the only men who are ever in my bed, they, and You, are enough.*"

Yet God took her by surprise and brought Don—a godly man and the representation of everything she'd ever wanted—into her life. Both she and Don were delightfully overwhelmed that God would allow them to find love again. Neither of them had anticipated nor sought to marry again. They each were dedicated to loving Jesus only. And having found each other they were excited at the prospect of serving God together if He led them to be married.

But pride often goes before the fall, Barbara admitted.

She and Don were newly engaged, and he was going to be leaving town with his adult sons for some father-son time together. Barbara recalled what happened next.

"When I discovered in a phone call that Don hadn't yet told his ex-wife that we were engaged, my mind started racing here and there about her finding out from her sons, and not from my fiancé, that we were engaged and showing up on their trip to try to win Don back. Nothing could've been further from the truth, but I suddenly became fragile and an emotional mess over all of it. I hung up the phone, angry at my fiancé, and went for a run, which is what I'd do back then to clear my head.

"Of course, I started out with angry words inside my head: *I'm reestablishing my independence. I don't need anyone anyway. Who cares about being alone. I was fine and had everything I needed before I met him and I can be that again.* And then it dawned on me (or perhaps the Holy Spirit enlightened me) that I'd transferred my emotional dependence from my Bridegroom Jesus to this man of flesh.

"I'd become chick-like* in the way I handled the conversation with him, which I'm sure left that man on the other end of the phone wondering what he was getting himself into with this woman he suddenly didn't recognize.

"I returned home and called Don to apologize. I told him that I realized I had transferred my emotional dependence away from my Lord and on to him. I acknowledged my behavior came from what is called 'old tapes' from a previous relationship. By admitting to Don what I'd done, we grew closer because Don knew I had the tools from my life experience and my walk with Jesus to realize I couldn't go to him for solutions—which relieved him of the burden to solve things for me."

Fortunately for both of them, Barbara realized what she'd done and corrected the situation. Looking back on that incident years later, Don

---

* Barbara described "chick-like" as whiny and emotionally immature.

told his wife, "I am so fortunate that you saw yourself in that moment. Or better, that God revealed that to you. Things could have turned out very differently."

By transferring her emotional dependence from God to her husband, Barbara was taking away Don's breathing room. She was putting pressure on him that he wasn't meant to bear, suffocating him in a sense. When she remembered that her true Husband, the Lord Jesus Christ, was the only One who could fill her insecurities and bring peace to her anxieties, and she actually admitted it to her now-husband, she was giving him room to breathe again.

When you and I look to God—not our husbands—to meet our emotional needs, it frees them to be the men God created them to be. I like to think it gives them breathing room. It allows them to decompress and think straight and desire our presence again. And it allows us time to sort through our emotions and gain a proper, God-honoring perspective.

When you and I look to God—not our husbands—to meet our emotional needs, it frees them to be the men God created them to be.

What Not to Do

Any wife can suck the life out of her husband through her emotional insecurities. She can drain him dry through constant talk about finances, her fears and failures, her anxieties, her weight, her poor body image, or whatever is stressing her out at the moment. I just did that to my husband this morning.

Any wife can suck the life out of her husband through her emotional insecurities.

In addition to being a pastor, Hugh keeps a second job as a city parks and trails ranger to help us make financial ends meet. For the most part he enjoys the job, until every June when his wife comes unglued because the city's Human Resources Department cuts all the part-time rangers' hours in half so it can meet its fiscal year-end budget. This morning, as I do each June, I transferred my financial dependence on God to my husband and expected him to give me the peace of mind and the assurance that we would be able to meet *our* monthly budget in light of the city's action again. I should have remembered *God* is the One who stretches our dollars each month, not my husband. *God* is ultimately the One who provides for us, even when it doesn't look on paper like every bill will be paid. And I can confidently say, after apologizing to my husband and bringing the matter to God in prayer, that *God* will once again take care of this matter. My meltdown was a result of emotionally reacting to a situation without taking it to my spiritual Husband first and letting Him filter out my feelings, fears, and anxieties. The result of my meltdown was that I sucked the life and enthusiasm out of my husband's morning and ended up with yet another example for this book of what *not* to do.*

How to Be Peace-Filled, Not Stress-Filled

The Bible gives us instructions on how to be calm and peace-filled, rather than stressed-out and worried about life's circumstances. This biblical instruction is great advice for wives (like me) who tend to go to their husbands to solve the problems and anxieties that are plaguing them. By following this advice, we can not only breathe better ourselves, but we can help give our husbands breathing room as well.

In Philippians 4:6-7 we are commanded:

> Do not be anxious about anything, but in every situation, by prayer and petition, with thanksgiving, present your requests to God. And the peace of God, which transcends

---

* That should be my next series of books: *What Not to Do: Lessons I've Learned the Hard Way* by Cindi McMenamin. My daughter is convinced I should already be writing *What Not to Wear* because of the '80s-like colors and '90s-like prints I pull out of my closet and put on every day!

> all understanding, will guard your hearts and your minds in Christ Jesus.

I especially like those instructions in the New Living Translation because they are so straight and to the point:

> Don't worry about anything; instead, pray about everything. Tell God what you need, and thank him for all he has done. Then you will experience God's peace, which exceeds anything we can understand. His peace will guard your hearts and minds as you live in Christ Jesus.

In other words, instead of worrying about it, pray about it, thank God ahead of time for how He chooses to take care of it, and experience His peace. Just in case you didn't get that, here it is, for the *fourth* time in a four-point process:

1. Don't worry.
2. Pray about it.
3. Thank God ahead of time for dealing with it.
4. Experience His unfathomable peace that will guard your heart and mind.

These are things we can do to guard our minds with peace so we don't lay unnecessary stress on our husbands. Pray about what concerns you instead of smothering him with it. Then you both will be able to breathe a lot easier.

Create the Space

Transferring your emotional dependence to God and praying about your concerns are just the beginning steps to giving your husband room to breathe. Here are more ways to create emotional and physical space for him.

Lower Your Expectations

This is a huge one. And I don't mean settle for less. I simply mean that every woman has expectations when she marries. High expectations. And then later she either raises them, refuses to lower them, or loses them altogether. But when you keep in mind that your husband is a man, not God, that he has his faults like you, and that he operates well after being fed and having time to relax, you won't be as disappointed.

I know you don't consciously expect your husband to be God, but we all look to someone or something to fill us, calm us, and comfort us. Barbara said the day she called Don and apologized for transferring her dependence from God to him became one of the touchstones in her life of the past 20 years. "I know when I get 'chick-like' that I've transferred my emotional dependence on him; that's not fair to him, and it's an insult to my Lord."

When we expect our husbands to come through for us like God would, they will disappoint us every time. And no husband wants to disappoint his wife. So don't set him up for failure. Keep yourself in check emotionally by asking yourself often, "Who is the one I am ultimately depending on?" If the answer to that question is anyone other than God (yourself included!), confess your misaligned priorities and invite God back onto the throne of your life. It will keep you and your husband breathing easier.

When we expect our husbands to come through for us like God would, they will disappoint us every time.

Lighten Up with the List

Every man is familiar with the "Honey-Do List" ("Honey, will you do this for me?"). The list usually includes household repairs, delegated responsibilities with the kids, things to pick up from the store on their way home, and so on. Most men expect to be given this list. Some even, bless their hearts, *ask* for it. (These must be men who consider "acts of service" their love language. If you're married to one, don't knock it. It means he actually loves doing those things because it's his way of showing you that he loves you.) But no man wants to come home to a list shoved in his face. And once he has his list, he needs a little breathing room to accomplish the items on it.

One man told me, "When my wife says, 'Are you going to do it now?' or 'When are you going to get that done?' she sees it as reminding me. I do need a reminder now and then, but I can tend to see her continual asking as nagging. I wish she'd trust me to do it once I've had some time to relax and enjoy some downtime."

Leave It for Later

Allison wisely learned in her early years of marriage not to launch into big discussions or problems with her husband right when they reunited after a long day or upon the heels of his return from a business trip. "It really helps to take some time to get readjusted and caught up and to wait awhile before dumping the big issues on him. He not only needs the breather, but everything looks better (for both of us) after a nice dinner together, or even a good night's sleep!"

Let Him Relax

Another way to let him breathe is to let him relax.

Judy, whose story is in chapter 3, said, "Sometimes it bothers me when Monte spends a couple of hours in front of the TV when he gets home from work or on weekends. But then I remember he's older now, he's worked hard, and he needs that time to relax. Sometimes I'll sit there with him, if I sense he'd like me there. And sometimes I let him have his 'veg' time if I sense he just needs to be alone."

Avoid the "Big 3"

Several years ago I interviewed 50 husbands who had been married anywhere from 5 to 50 years and asked them what they needed most from their wives. I included their input in my book *When a Woman Inspires Her Husband*. One of the chapters in that book reminded wives of a few actions of ours that tend to drive our men crazy: smothering, mothering, and hovering. Don't be guilty of any of them.

Stop the Smothering

We can smother our husbands when we feel the need to be with them at every waking moment or when we feel the need to talk with them about everything. Barbara said "no chick chat" should be a rule of thumb so we don't unknowingly smother our husbands. There's a reason it's called "chick chat." It's the kind of talk we would engage in with our girlfriends. Ladies, your husband probably isn't interested in what happened at the mall, what that shampoo is doing to your hair, or how many calories you saved by making better choices at lunchtime. Save those things for your girlfriends, who really do want to hear about them and share their experiences too.

My good friend Connie said she has a tendency to smother her husband of ten years, Tyler, by constantly asking, "Do you miss me?" It's mainly a joke, but she's found it's much better when he offers on his own that he misses her than when she tries to pull it out of him.

Typically, your man needs his space more than you need yours. One husband told his wife, "I love that you want to remain physically close to me after we've been physically intimate, but I need to regain my space for a few minutes and then my heart wants to be back with you again." If your man feels the need to be separated from you, just for a bit, after being physically intimate, *how much more* does he need his space if he's been working alongside you, answering to you, helping you, or listening to you all day? Give him enough physical space to want to be near you again.

Now if your husband is the one who wants to talk about everything and be right next to you at all times, and you are the one who typically needs your space, talk with him about ways each of you can have your needed space yet still feel connected to one another. The important thing is knowing what *your* man wants and needs so that neither of you feel smothered.

Typically, your man needs his space more than you need yours.

Cut the Mothering

Every man wants a girlfriend, not a mother. So act like his girlfriend, not the woman who raised him. Don't tell him things like, "Be careful" because that's what his mom would say. Say instead, "Have a great time, babe." Don't say, "Call me as soon as you get home." Instead, say, "Can't wait to hear how it goes." Don't say, "When are you going to take the trash out? I've told you three times and I'm not going to tell you again!" Try instead, "Hey, babe, do you mind helping me out and taking out that trash when you get a chance?"

Every man wants a girlfriend, not a mother. So act like his girlfriend, not the woman who raised him.

Do you get the idea? Talk to him like his lover, not his mother, and you'll not only be giving him breathing room but will be making him want less room between the two of you!

Halt the Hovering

You've heard of helicopter parents—those who hover over their children and never let them out of their sight, even when they're perfectly safe? Well, there are helicopter wives too. And they tend to drive their husbands crazy. Wives hover when they feel the need to oversee, supervise, make sure he's safe, or just be a part of his everything. Your man needs to know you trust him on his own, with the kids, with important decisions, and so on. Don't emasculate him by making him think you always have to be there to make sure things go well.

Just Breathe

When you give your husband emotional space by looking to God to be your all-in-all and letting your husband do what he can, you are saying, "I love you, but I'm not expecting you to be God." When you give him physical space, you are saying, "I trust you when I'm not around."

And when you continue to allow him to breathe, you just may find that you become a breath of fresh air that he is longing for once he's back in your presence.

PRAYING IT THROUGH

Lord, help me always look to You to be my First Love so I'm not laying an unfair burden on my husband that he was never meant to bear. Forgive me for going to him to do what only You can do for me. Help me to stop smothering, mothering, and hovering, and instead give my husband breathing room so he will find my love refreshing, never draining. Thank You, God, for giving me the insight to see when he needs his space and when I need to go to You for what I need. In Christ's name, amen.

YOUR FOCUS FOR THE WEEK

You can become a woman who is easier to live with and more enjoyable to be around when you give your husband breathing room. List below one or two ways you can give your husband physical or emotional space this week.

I will give my husband space this week by:

7

Light Him Up

Praising the Man God Created Him to Be

How handsome you are, my beloved!
Oh, how charming!

Song of Songs 1:16

You have stolen my heart, my sister, my bride;
you have stolen my heart
with one glance of your eyes.

Song of Songs 4:9

Picture a woman in love. She's got a sparkle in her eyes, a smile on her face, and a spring in her step. She's so optimistic about the future, you can't get her down. She's walking on air, feeling great, and losing weight!

But what does a man in love look like?

He isn't giddy like we can tend to be. He doesn't read your text messages to his guy friends or brag that he stole your heart away or show off his ring on Instagram!

According to my husband, and a few others, men in love smile more, they take better care of themselves by the way they dress and stay fit, they feel more adventurous and courageous and are willing to take more risks, and they walk a little taller. In fact, they *swagger*. (Yep, *swagger*. ALL of the men I interviewed used that exact word. It means they carry themselves more confidently. I believe that's male speak for "a spring in his step.")

When my brother, Steve, at 24, told me he had proposed to his dream girl, Sophie, I could hear in his voice how captivated he was by her. "There's something about her. She has a way of wrapping herself around the heart of everyone she meets." Now, when did that brother of mine get poetic? When he fell in love. Fifteen years later—after a mortgage, two kids, and a high-stress career—he still says the same thing about his dream girl. I believe it's because Sophie still knows how to "light him up."

The Power of a Wife

You, as your husband's wife, have the ability to light him up more than anyone else. Your compliments and praise can go further than anyone else's. Your pride in him is far more important to him than his mother's, or even his children's. He truly wants to know you think the world of him. And he wants the world to know it too.

Remember (from chapter 2) how the new bride talked of her husband in the Song of Songs? Well, her husband talked of her too, in a moving, intimate description in the fourth chapter of the Song. Solomon—a man in love—described his beloved with song lyrics that sound like a cross between Shakespeare and a John Mayer song! I love how the Bible boldly and unashamedly, through the words of Solomon, tells it like it is when it comes to what turns on a man. Don't mean to make you blush, but here are some of the highlights of that song that Solomon sang to his new bride (I've mixed a couple of contemporary translations that sound more like how a man would talk—or sing—today):

> You're so beautiful, my darling,
> so beautiful, and your dove eyes are veiled
> By your hair as it flows and shimmers,
> like a flock of goats in the distance
> streaming down a hillside in the sunshine.
> Your smile is generous and full—
> expressive and strong and clean.

Your lips are jewel red,
your mouth elegant and inviting,
your veiled cheeks soft and radiant.
The smooth, lithe lines of your neck
command notice—all heads turn in awe and admiration!
Your breasts are like fawns,
twins of a gazelle, grazing among the first spring flowers.

The sweet, fragrant curves of your body,
the soft, spiced contours of your flesh
Invite me, and I come. I stay
until dawn breathes its light and night slips away.
You're beautiful from head to toe, my dear love,
beautiful beyond compare, absolutely flawless.

You've captured my heart, dear friend.
You looked at me, and I fell in love.
One look my way and I was hopelessly in love!
How beautiful your love, dear, dear friend—
far more pleasing than a fine, rare wine,
your fragrance more exotic than select spices.
The kisses of your lips are honey, my love,
every syllable you speak a delicacy to savor.
Your clothes smell like the wild outdoors,
the ozone scent of high mountains.
Dear lover and friend, you're a secret garden,
a private and pure fountain.
Body and soul, you are paradise,
a whole orchard of succulent fruits—
(Song of Songs 4:1-7,9-13 MSG).

You are a spring in the garden,
a fountain of pure water,
and a refreshing stream
from Mount Lebanon (Song of Songs 4:15 CEV).

The Allure of a Woman

In that passage Solomon was saying he was captivated by his bride's

- eyes
- long, flowing hair
- radiant smile
- white teeth
- soft lips (red, no doubt! What man doesn't like red lipstick?)
- soft, blushing cheeks
- long, smooth neck
- shapely breasts
- sweet, fragrant perfume
- feminine curves
- soft, smooth skin
- inviting looks with her eyes
- sweet kisses
- soft voice
- soft clothing
- tantalizing perfume

Did you notice that in this description Solomon started at the top of his wife's head, describing her eyes through her veil and her flowing hair, then followed her neck to her breasts, then her feminine curves, and finally in verse 7 he summarized his treasure:

> You're beautiful from head to toe, my dear love,
> beautiful beyond compare, absolutely flawless (MSG).

Later, in chapter 7 of The Song, Solomon described her again but started at her feet and moved up her body to her nose and forehead! Listen to his poetic expression of what he saw:

> You are a princess,
> and your feet are graceful
> in their sandals.

Your thighs are works of art,
each one a jewel;
your navel is a wine glass
filled to overflowing.
Your body is full and slender
like a bundle of wheat
bound together by lilies.
Your breasts are like twins
of a deer.
Your neck is like ivory,
and your eyes sparkle
like the pools of Heshbon
by the gate of Bath-Rabbim.
Your nose is beautiful
like Mount Lebanon
above the city of Damascus.
Your head is held high
like Mount Carmel;
your hair is so lovely
it holds a king prisoner.

You are beautiful,
so very desirable!
You are tall and slender
like a palm tree,
and your breasts are full.
I will climb that tree
and cling to its branches.
I will discover that your breasts
are clusters of grapes,
and that your breath
is the aroma of apples.
Kissing you is more delicious
than drinking the finest wine.
How wonderful and tasty! (Song of Songs 7:1-9 CEV).

I believe the Bible recorded Solomon's intimate observations of his wife as a reinforcement to us of the good and pure aspect of sexuality within the context of marriage, and to underscore to us the importance of a man's sexual pleasure with his own wife! There was no lust in this scenario, no coveting a woman who was not his own. Solomon was being the man God created him to be and desiring what he was designed to desire.

It is a fact that men are visually stimulated. It is wired into your husband's DNA to want nothing more than to watch you and study every inch of you. And even better than that is if he knows *you* enjoy being watched and studied too!

The really delightful and applicable part of Song 7, after Solomon described his wife from the toes up, is how enthusiastically she responded to his verbal detailing of her anatomy and his affirmation of her beauty:

> My darling, I am yours,
> and you desire me...
> I will give you my love...
> I have stored up for you
> all kinds of tasty fruits (Song of Songs 7:10-13 CEV).

I'm guessing there may be some wives reading this who feel uncomfortable at the thought of their husbands studying them. Our own body insecurities make us feel critical of ourselves, and we naturally assume our husbands will be just as critical. If you are one who insists that the lights stay off when you're undressed, let me assure you of this: Your husband isn't half as critical of you as you are of yourself. Men see in soft focus. Seriously. They are usually just so happy to see their wife naked that they're not going through their list of what they wish you looked like. You and I keep that list about ourselves. I'm pretty certain our husbands don't.

Our own body insecurities make us feel critical of ourselves, and we naturally assume our husbands will be just as critical.

Granted, the more confident you are in how you look, the more you will let your husband feast his eyes on you. But if you are not confident and at ease with your husband sexually, your inhibition could lead him down a path of temptation that can easily turn into an addiction.

The Danger of Inhibition

The staggering statistics on the percentage of men who view pornography (Christian men included, and even a high percentage of pastors!) attest to the fact that men are visually stimulated to a fault. And please let me say, as gently as I can, that if you aren't letting your man see you and admire you in a playful, alluring, teasing, and sensual way, you are leaving a door open for him to want to see the female body somewhere else. That is not to say you are the cause of your husband wanting to view pornographic material. Believe it or not, most men were first exposed to porn between the ages of nine and twelve, and although it started out as curiosity, the more repressed a man is sexually (due to a wife who sees sex as shameful or uncomfortable in any way), the more tempted he is to fulfill that strong desire through porn. Add to that the power of visual stimulation, and many men can easily become addicted to it.

I realize women can be sexually inhibited and feel that sex is shameful because of past abuse. If that is your situation, please consider personal counseling as well as marital counseling with your husband. Counseling can help you open up and deal with issues that may be negatively affecting your view of sex and, ultimately, your sex life with your husband. And God can, through that counseling, redeem and restore your view of sex, and even use your husband's unconditional love and acceptance of you to help heal that area in your heart.

Because your husband can't help how he is wired, can't help the fact that he has a strong sexual desire that is triggered visually, *you* be the one he watches and admires. *You* be the one he can freely see and touch. *You* be his real-life fantasy girl. You certainly don't need to have the perfect body to be all of that. None of us is perfect. And none of us should ever feel that we have to compete with airbrushed or computer-generated images that will always appear better than the real thing. You just need to have a perfectly open attitude and willingness to be pleasing to his eyes. Pray for a positive view of your body that God's Word says is "fearfully and wonderfully made" (Psalm 139:14).

One phrase that will light up your husband probably more than any other is if you tell him, "Let me be your fantasy girl." Believe me, he wants to be *right* in his desires, imagination, and mentally stored images. There is so much visual stimulation for your husband on television, in movies, and in pornography that is just a click away on a computer, iPad, iPhone, or smartphone that he is constantly bombarded with the temptation to look. (I don't have to know your husband to make a statement like that. It's pretty much universal to the male species.) Be aware that he is a man, and therefore he has a desire to *see* what is beautiful, what is sexually arousing, what is pleasing to his eyes. God made your man that way so he would desire *you*, his wife. So again, *you* be the object of his desire. *You* be the one he fantasizes about. *You* be the one he keeps mental images stored in his mind about. You, as his wife, are the *only one* he can look at, fantasize about, touch, and be intimate with emotionally and physically, and still be right before God. That means you hold a large piece to making it easy or difficult for him to be obedient to God.

You, as his wife, are the only one *he can look at, fantasize about, touch, and be intimate with emotionally and physically, and still be right before God.*

Now again, please don't think I'm saying you are in any way responsible for your man's straying eyes or heart. He has to make his own choice to be obedient to God and faithful to his wife. But as far as it depends on you, don't give him *any* reason to be tempted to look at or want anything or anyone else.

Now that you see what delights a man, you have an idea of what you have physically that lights him up sexually and builds his confidence as a man. Now let's look at what that new bride in Song of Songs said to her husband to *audibly* arouse him. It lends itself to a beautiful lesson in how our words can build up our husbands and make them feel like stronger, more masculine, and more desirable men.

The Power of Your Words

The new wife we looked at in chapter 2 had eyes for her husband as you and I once had eyes for ours (and hopefully still do). She praised him. And he ate it up.

Listen to the creative ways she told him he was wonderful.

> Kiss me tenderly!
> Your love is better than wine,
>   and you smell so sweet.
> All the young women adore you;
> the very mention of your name
>   is like spreading perfume (Song of Songs 1:2-3 CEV).

> Take me away with you! Let's run off together!
>   An elopement with my King-Lover!
> We'll celebrate, we'll sing,
>   we'll make great music.
> Yes! For your love is better than vintage wine.
>   Everyone loves you—of course! And why not?
> (Song of Songs 1:4 MSG).

> My love, you are handsome,
>   truly handsome—
> the fresh green grass
>   will be our wedding bed
> in the shade of cedar
>   and cypress trees (Song of Songs 1:16-17 CEV).

> And you, my love,
> are an apple tree
>   among trees of the forest.

Your shade brought me pleasure;
your fruit was sweet.
You led me to your banquet room
and showered me with love.
Refresh and strengthen me
with raisins and apples.
I am hungry for love!
Put your left hand under my head
and embrace me
with your right arm (Song of Songs 2:3-6 CEV).

My darling, I am yours,
and you are mine,
as you feed your sheep
among the lilies.
Pretend to be a young deer
dancing on mountain slopes
until daylight comes
and shadows fade away (Song of Songs 2:16-17 CEV).

Let's summarize what this new bride said in Song 1 and 2 that really resonated with her husband's heart. But lest it sound like material for a nice G-rated adult Sunday school class for married couples, let me take the liberty of paraphrasing what this wife said to her husband in the way we would *really* talk to our husbands today. (This might not be the way *you* would talk to your husband, but it's most likely what he would want to hear you say, and what I believe this wife was actually saying way back then in the unedited, uncensored, un-"tone-it-down" version of the original Hebrew manuscript.) Trust me, these are the words (paraphrased from this passage of Scripture) that your husband wants to hear from *you*:

- "Kiss me—full on the mouth!" (Song of Songs 1:2 MSG).
- "Your love is intoxicating."
- "You smell incredible. In fact, your scent drives me crazy!"
- "Any woman would be crazy not to think you are *The Man*."

- "Let's run off together—now!"
- "Let's enjoy a private party for two!"
- "Any woman would love to be with you. How did I get so lucky?"
- "When you lie next to me, all my senses come alive and I'm so ready for you!"
- "You are so hot."
- "I can't wait to get you into bed!" (Hey, go back and read it for yourself. I'm not making this up!)
- "You stand head and shoulders above everyone else in everything you do."
- "I can't wait to be with you."
- "You sure spoiled me tonight."
- "I crave your body next to mine."
- "I want you."
- "I'm yours, you're mine—there are no limits or boundaries."
- "Explore me thoroughly. Let me be your adventure."

You were designed by God, body and soul, to drink of your husband's love deeply. So build him up sexually. Make him feel confident by assuring him you love how he looks, what he does, what he feels like, and ultimately who he is. The more you do this, the more freedom he will have to intimately express his love toward you.

Make him feel confident by assuring him you love how he looks, what he does, what he feels like, and ultimately who he is.

Talk Him Up

Another way to light up your husband is to talk him up.

Steve said this about his wife, Sophie: "She talks me up when I'm not around, even if we're in a fight. She is especially mindful of boosting my confidence before I have a big meeting or interview where I may not be as confident as I need to be."

Barbara realized that when she heaps praise upon her husband, Don, he stands a little taller.

"My number one ministry is to Don as his wife, so everything I do and make decisions about is based on that perspective," Barbara said. "His gift, his reputation, his calling, the 'work' God gave him to do is ever present in all discussions. Like when he might say, 'I wish I could give you a big house,' or 'I wish I had a photographic memory,' or when he compares himself to a successful salesperson/businessman, I *always* mention how they can't read Greek or Hebrew, that God didn't give them a calling and ministry with the value of his, that he is The Best Salesperson because God gave him something intangible to 'sell' and he keeps after it. I highlight his strengths repeatedly. And when he speaks, I never take my eyes off him to make sure anyone watching knows how important he is and how valuable his words are to me. Oh, and I never correct him in public."

Emily, whom we met in chapter 3, learned that her husband, George, is also a man who thrives on words of affirmation.

"He loves when I praise him or voice appreciation for something he has done," Emily said. "Early in our marriage when we would be with friends I would sometimes tease or put down George. I wasn't aware that this really hurt him. We had some conversations about it, and I realized I needed to be more respectful toward him. So I try my best to praise George when we are with others and not to put him down or embarrass him. These words of affirmation uplift him and make him more trusting and understanding toward me.

"I now focus on showing him respect and I find those things he is great at and celebrate him."

Emily said, "Everyone loves to hear that they have done something well, and it's even better when the words are coming from your loved one whom you are constantly trying to please."

My friend Dawn Marie Wilson, an author, blogger, and pastor's wife who helps women make better choices to upgrade their lives, marriage, and parenting, also noticed how her words make her husband of almost 45 years, Bob, beam: "My husband's most recent project is landscaping our front yard. It's grueling, dirty work, and I keep dishing out the praise. Lavish praise! He may be exhausted at the end of the day, but he always stands a little taller when I admire his muscles or when he hears me tell a neighbor, 'I'm so glad I married a handyman!'"

Build Him Up

In Song 4:11, the Shulamite bride talked up her husband by telling him what she loved about him.

Julie Gorman, author of the book *What I Wish My Mother Had Told Me About Men*, said, "Every, yes, *every* day, I ask myself, *How can I add value to Greg? How can I express my respect to him in such a way that he feels it?*"

Allison offered this advice to build up your husband: "Guard your words so that you only say positive things about him in public. Even praise him by saying something you appreciate about him in front of him and other people. Showing esteem for your husband is a powerful thing—and it sends a powerful message of love and respect to your husband, as well as others.

"Then, in private, you do not always have to say what is on your mind. Erring on the side of kindness always wins. Let God guard your words. You can't take them back."

Ephesians 4:29 says, "Let everything you say be good and helpful, so that your words will be an encouragement to those who hear them" (NLT).

In order to truly practice Ephesians 4:29 with our husbands we need to learn how to reframe what we say.

Frame It Well

How often do you and your spouse end up at odds because you said something (or he said something) that didn't come out quite right?

How we frame our questions or statements can make all the difference in the world.

How we frame our questions or statements can make all the difference in the world.

Consider the following scenario: You are getting ready to go out and grab an inexpensive dinner with your husband. But you feel like showering first and looking nice—you want it to feel like a date, and you are doing it for him. But he is focused on food. And he's hungry. You put on a cute dress and fix your hair and makeup as he patiently waits for you. Then, when you're finally ready, you see he's wearing his favorite T-shirt and his comfy but not-so-attractive shorts and say, "Are you going to go dressed like *that*?" You meant, "I dressed nicely. You didn't." He hears, "You look like a slob."

So you try again: "I dressed up for *you*."

He hears, "I dressed up for *you*" but doesn't know how he's supposed to respond. *Is that an accusation that I didn't dress up for her? Is she waiting for a "thank you" or a "you look great"? Is she expecting me to wear something else? What am I supposed to do?*

He ends up opting for, "Is that new?" (thinking maybe it is and you'll be upset if he doesn't notice).

You hear, "Did you spend money again on clothes that you don't need?"

Now, do you see where all of this misunderstanding and defensiveness can lead? Your man shouldn't have to walk through a minefield to get out the door to have dinner with his wife. Yet the bombs can go off when we say something explosive that we didn't think to carefully frame.

We can talk to our husbands without offending, confusing, or putting them on the defensive by framing what we say into a compliment and eliminating their guesswork.

I put together a chart of the things wives often want to say to their husbands along with a suggested way to frame them well.

What We Want to Say	A Better Way to Frame It
Are you going to go dressed like that?	Why don't you wear that new shirt? You look terrific in it.
I wish you'd open doors for me like you used to.	I really like when you open doors for me. It shows me you care.
I tried calling you. You never called back.	Was everything okay today? I wanted to connect by phone and see how you were doing.
We're $400 short this month.	I was able to save $100 in coupons this month, which will help toward our deficit.
We need to talk.	Let me know when you have a minute so we can talk about ________.
Why don't we go out on dates anymore?	I miss spending time with you.
Why don't we have sex as often as we used to?	I look forward to spending some intimate time with you.
Have you been putting on some weight?	How about we go for a short walk tonight after dinner?
Why do we always have to watch what *you* want to see?	Let's pick out a new movie together.
We've been eating out too much.	I'd like to cook something special for you tonight.
We haven't gone away together in a long time.	Wouldn't it be great to get away somewhere together? If you let me know your availability, I'll plan something special for the two of us.

Did you notice something about how all of those statements were reworded? The statements in the left column sounded like accusations. They were pointed questions that can put your spouse on the defensive. But by reframing them, the questions turned into compliments and what might have been perceived as an accusation turned into a form of admiration.

Look again at the questions and statements on the left side of that chart. If you would never want to hear your husband ask you something like, "Are you going to wear *that*?" or "Have you gained a little weight lately?" or "I wish you looked and acted more like you did back when we met," then why would you say it to him? Speak to your man in a complimentary manner rather than in a negative tone. And make sure you watch your body language. (My husband does *not* like when I say something to him with my hands on my hips. For me, it's just a comfortable way to stand. To him, it says I'm assuming command of the USS *Enterprise*!)

PRAYING IT THROUGH

Do you realize you are the only one who can light up your husband and thrill his senses and allow him pleasure in a way that pleases the heart of God? Do you realize your words can build him up like no other's? As you seek to light him up you are fulfilling your God-appointed role as his wife and ministering to him in a way that no one else truly can. So start reframing your words, building him up, and turning him on so you can once again be the sparkle in his eyes, the woman behind his smile, and the stagger in his walk.

> *Help me, dear Lord, to be the light in my husband's life and the wind beneath his wings. Daily remind me that I hold the power to build him up or tear him down. I want to please You by pleasing him, so give me discernment to know when to speak, when to touch, and when to just silently love him. In the name of Jesus, amen.*

YOUR FOCUS FOR THE WEEK

Every day this week ask yourself these two questions:

1. How can I reframe this statement or question to build him up rather than deflate him?
2. How can I show him, through words or touch, that he's still *The Man*?

8

Close the Gap

Steering Clear of the Emotional Cave

I will search for the one my heart loves.

Song of Songs 3:2

Misty described for me the gap in her marriage. It sounded typical of the e-mails I receive from wives seeking to reconnect with their husbands.

"Over the years my husband has drifted from me, but perhaps I have drifted from him," Misty wrote. "My husband is a wonderful man, full of life, never complains, and he is a loyal employee. He just doesn't know how to be 'one flesh.'

"He has lived an honest and honorable life, but he sometimes forgets he has a wife who wants to know his deepest thoughts and connect with him. I would describe him as 'aloof.' He has the best intentions and he is very sweet, however he floats around in his own world most of the time. Thirty-five years in the military and constantly moving around made it difficult for him to make deep lasting friends, thus he is a loner.

"He and I differ, too, in how we relate to God. And even when my husband is home, sometimes I don't feel connected to him emotionally. One of the things I have done to connect with him is turn the TV off during mealtimes. We sit face-to-face and talk about the day. I also tell him how important it is for him to have my back when I am struggling with something—whether it is a work stressor, a physical ailment, or a personal matter. I also try to lead by example and show him how much I support him in all he does. I use the phrase, 'We are one flesh. What you do affects me and vice versa.' I especially point this out when it comes to taking care of our health and making friends with other Christian couples."

Signs of the Gap

I noticed seven statements of Misty's that typically contribute to "the gap"—a feeling of distance between husbands and wives:

- My husband has drifted from me, but perhaps I have drifted from him.
- He just doesn't know how to be "one flesh."
- I would describe him as "aloof."
- He floats around in his own world most of the time.
- He is a loner.
- He and I differ in how we relate to God.
- Even when he is home, sometimes I don't feel connected to him emotionally.

To be honest, there are days several of those statements would describe my husband too. And many other women's. And maybe even yours. But in all fairness, there are days when Hugh could say that several of those statements describe me.

We all have our days. We all have our personalities and lifestyles. The bottom line is that through the years distance can grow between husbands and wives. Anyone will tell you it's likely. But I will tell you it's not inevitable.

The Seriousness of It

The number one cause for divorce today is *lack of communication.*[1] Seriously. Just a decade ago it was adultery, but today failing to communicate, communicating poorly, or just letting the emotional gap widen between a husband and wife can be most fatal to marriages.

The number one cause for divorce today is lack of communication.

Because of the differences between you and your husband—your different personalities, different upbringings, different ways you approach life—you have enough of a gap between you to start with. But when one of you goes into your emotional cave instead of communicating and leaves the other to deal with the feeling of being shut out, that gap widens even more. Whether it's you who retreats emotionally or your husband (or *both* of you), let's look at healthy alternatives to emotional withdrawal and ways we can keep connected so the gap between you and your husband isn't allowed to widen.

Finding the Key

To this day, Hugh will readily admit he is not the verbal communicator in our marriage. I am. But just because I'm a writer and a speaker, and therefore a communicator by profession, does not necessarily mean I communicate well with *him.* In fact, because I know how to communicate in general, I figured I had it made. *I can make any man talk. I can sort through anything by just talking about it,* I thought. I was so wrong.

We both have had to figure out how to communicate well with *each other.*

Hugh may be an "under communicator" when it comes to our marriage. But I happen to have a problem called "over-communicating" that can be just as deadly. Seriously, it would probably drive *any* man batty. Put the under- and over-communicator together and you have one man dying for some silence and one woman trying to squeeze a few more words out of her non-talker. I tell you that story only to underscore the point that communication REALLY IS key to your marriage.

- Communication is key to a great sex life—being able to talk with one another about what you like and dislike.
- Communication is key to humility—being able to admit when you're wrong and ask for forgiveness.
- Communication is key to forgiveness—being able to let go of offenses and receive another's apology.
- Communication is key to emotional intimacy—being able to ask questions, listen, and say what each of you needs to hear in order to trust each other and let your guards down.
- Communication is key to trust—being honest and open about what you are feeling and experiencing.
- Communication is key to appreciating the differences in your spouse. You can't understand what you don't talk about.

The importance of good communication cannot be overstated. It is what *closes the gap* between you and your husband.

Communication is what closes the gap *between you and your husband.*

Widening the Gap

There were some women in the Bible who weren't careful in how they communicated with their husbands, and they suffered for it by creating a gap in their marriage from which they never really recovered.

Rachel—whose love story with Jacob is recorded in Genesis 29—apparently lacked communication skills with her husband. Or at least she had her failing moments like we all do. Heartbroken at not being able to have a child, she let her jealousy of her older sister's children (her sister, Leah, was also married to Jacob), and frustration at not being able to get pregnant herself, lead to an angry outburst and to the demand of her husband: "Give me children, or I'll die!" (Genesis 30:1). *Really, Rachel? Isn't that a bit dramatic? And is that going to make your husband want to work with you to solve the problem?*

Jacob's response was fraught with anger and rebuke. Scripture says, "Jacob became angry with her and said, 'Am I in the place of God, who has kept you from having children?'" (Genesis 30:2).

Rachel either expected her husband to be God and solve her problem (as some wives do) or she was in the mood to blame, accuse, and demand. That is not constructive communication. That is creating conflict.

What Rachel did next not only created a huge gap in the intimacy between her and Jacob, but it sent her into a wrestling match with her sister to compete for who could have the most babies. Rachel insisted her husband sleep with her maid so Rachel could feel like she was having children through her maidservant.

What if Rachel had talked lovingly with Jacob and told him she was feeling she had failed him because she didn't have children? What if she had tried to explain how unfulfilled she felt because her sister had several children and she had none? What if she had thought through her ridiculous demand and then chosen, instead, to clarify to Jacob that she didn't expect him to fix the situation, but just needed him to hold her, and comfort her, and pray for her that God would allow her to have children. What if she were to say, "I have your love, and it means so much to me. Pray that I will be content with that and not be so desperate to have more"?

Perhaps if she had talked with her husband about what she was feeling, he could've reinforced to her how very much she was loved and directed her back to Yahweh...the One who loved her as well and who can do all things in His perfect timing. Maybe they could've even prayed about it together. All we know is years later, Rachel finally called upon God for help, and it was then that she was able to conceive (Genesis 30:22-24).

The Ravages of Resentment

In 2 Samuel 6, we read that Michal, the wife of King David, resented her husband in her heart when she saw him through the palace window dancing in just his loin cloth as the ark of the covenant was being brought back to Jerusalem. (For the king of Israel to dance in a loin cloth through the streets of Jerusalem in a time when men were much more heavily clothed than they are today would be the equivalent, I suppose, of a megachurch pastor leaping and dancing down the aisle on a Sunday morning wearing only a Speedo! Okay, maybe ten times more intense!) But rather than first greeting him after a long trip and then eventually—maybe after dinner—sitting down with him and calmly saying, "I was a little concerned to see you dancing before the women in your underwear this morning. I would love to know what you were thinking," Michal "despised him in her heart" when she witnessed the event (verse 16). And as soon as she saw him—after a long leave of absence in which he was victoriously leading his armies at war—instead of giving him a hero's welcome, or an endearing hug because she had missed him, she accused him of being lowly and vulgar and publicly humiliating himself.

Had she been careful to investigate his heart on the matter, she would have learned that her husband was so enraptured by what God had done for the armies of Israel, and so elated to see the ark of the covenant returned to Jerusalem, that his humiliation was so that God could be glorified. He might've even told her, "Michal, today wasn't about me or even *you*, it was about celebrating the mighty works God has done!"

Because Michal accused her husband rather than communicated with him, a huge gap was created between her and David that day that never closed. Shortly after that incident she was given to another man (the equivalent of a forced divorce), and Scripture tells us God closed her womb and she was never able to conceive a child. God didn't take it lightly that she despised her husband in her heart and closed off from him.

What's at the Core?

Robin Reinke, my counselor-friend whom I referred to in chapter

4, says "emotional disconnect" is the primary reason wives don't experience more trust, passion, and communication with their husbands.

"Emotional disconnect" is the primary reason wives don't experience more trust, passion, and communication with their husbands.

What causes emotional disconnect?

"When your heart gets poked, it starts to close," Robin said. "And then it can get hardened. And yet if we learn how to repair and how to heal, we can emotionally reconnect with our spouse. First we have to develop an awareness of what is causing us to close off from our spouse."

In chapter 4 we talked about the pain that all of us have experienced and how we, as wounded people, filter our life's experiences through that grid of pain and sometimes end up seeing our spouse—rather than an unhealed issue in our lives—as the problem. Robin said in her own marriage, closing the gap came down to understanding what first caused her own pain and then developing a greater understanding of what caused her husband's pain and working to communicate and become reliably connected.

"What has been revolutionary for our marriage is when I had discovered the lies that had been planted in my heart that at times make me feel alone, unsafe, and rejected, and combat those with the truth that in Christ I am never alone, I'm safe, and I'm chosen," she said. "When I realize the truth of my identity and Whose I am, then I have the capacity to turn toward my husband and have deeper empathy and understanding for where he's coming from."

"It has been only in the last eight years that I realized my husband felt that he didn't measure up and struggled, at times, with feelings of failure. A lot of our fights were ignited out of my husband interpreting things that I would say that would trigger his feeling that he was a failure. Now that I've discovered this is the issue, I am able to speak truth to him that would refute those lies in his heart by telling him that he is significant and greatly valued. This keeps his heart open to me and helps us keep emotionally connected."

Do you know what causes the gap between you and your husband?

You might say, "We fight all the time." But Robin says, "According to Dr. Terry Hargrave, you don't have 30 fights. You have *one* fight *30 different ways.* The core issues are usually the same. By identifying those issues, you can become aware of them and work through them."

Narrowing the Gap

Robin gave me some steps that I found extremely helpful in narrowing the gap with Hugh. I think you might find them helpful, too, in attempting to communicate with your husband:

Realize the deeper core wound that is driving the problem or fight. Instead of thinking, *My spouse is just an angry man*, say instead, "I had no idea that my husband struggled so much with feeling he was not succeeding in the relationship." Robin said, "What we focus on grows. If I'm focused on what my husband is doing wrong, that will grow. If I focus on the fact that he's a good guy, that will heighten my awareness to see that."

Resist the urge to be defensive, accusative, or angry at your husband's words, actions, or responses. Instead, be open and curious. Tell yourself, "My husband is a good person. He is loving and is maybe acting like a jerk right now, but what is going on with him?"

Reject the lies that get you off course and create division between you and your spouse. "Your husband's wounds aren't the only ones in play here," Robin said. "We (wives) get triggered by a situation or by certain words and then we believe *our* lies: *I am alone. I am devalued. I'm not appreciated. I'm not respected.* Combat those lies."

Receive the truth of who you are in Christ. Once you receive the truth you can be more emotionally regulated and attuned to your husband. John 8:32 tells us: "Then you will know the truth and the truth will set you free."

Focus on the Facts

Robin also practices focusing on the facts of a situation, rather than unpredictable feelings. In marriage, we experience hurts. So we need to be aware of our past wounds and how they cause us to react to our present situations. For instance, instead of focusing on my feelings that say, *I'm devalued* or *I'm alone*, I can focus on the truth that proclaims, *I am valued. I am loved. I am not alone.* Then I can have a new action and instead of getting anxious, withdrawing from, or lecturing my husband, I can get connected to my heart and say, "I realize when you said this I felt devalued and started to shut down, but now I realize I am valued and I can choose to be connected and get close to you."

Each of us has to feel safe in order to start moving toward the other person to close the gap. Our only safety is in our relationship with Jesus, where we understand who we are in His eyes. Jesus has to be our all in all. When we feel safe in *Him*, we can feel safe with others too.

Our only safety is in our relationship with Jesus.

Read Between His Lines

When it comes to communicating, men don't want to have to read between the lines. They want us to be direct with them, not to hint around or imply. "Just say it" is their motto. However, our husbands can speak in veiled language too. They have their own way of being vague or mysterious at times. And that's when we need to learn to read between *their* lines.

I have a history of reading the *wrong* thing between Hugh's lines. When I began writing this book, words my husband has said through the years started to resurface in my mind. Like the time Hugh spoke up in a church staff meeting and said, "In another life I would've liked to have been a monk." (Try not to take *that* personally, ladies! Does he want the quiet life apart from me or what?) Or when he was in his study applying online for a job for Adventures by Disney and he answered "no" to the question, "Do you have commitments or obligations at home that would prevent you from being away for six to nine months at a time?" (Uh, he has a wife who might like to see him now and then. And we are supposed to be enjoying our empty-nest years together right now!) These were situations I complained about at the time, but Hugh never really explained to me the context of what he was saying or what he was feeling that caused him to say such things. So I read the wrong words in between his lines (words like "He doesn't want to be around me" and "He's tired of me and wants his space") and buried those misunderstandings in my heart. Because we never hashed them out and because he's not big on clarifying (yet I'm big on assuming), I let some of those things close off my heart and start the gap-widening process between us.

Just recently those situations came to my mind again. Perhaps it was God's way of showing me that certain issues between us were not resolved. Perhaps the Holy Spirit was convicting my heart for needlessly hanging on to some hurts and allowing my heart to close off from Hugh in some ways. But instead of looking at pain in my life and asking, "What is causing me to react this way?" and then sharing what I discovered with Hugh, I brought those two issues up one night before bed in a machine gun-like assault. Hugh, the internal processor, looked shell-shocked and didn't say much in response (which tends to hurt me more). But two mornings later he wrote me a brief e-mail, expressing his heart. He was telling me, after all this time, how to *correctly* read between his lines. This is what he wrote:

> *Hi, Sweetie,*
>
> *Just wanted to share these words with you:*
>
> *Whenever I look for a job that includes travel (like when I was applying for Adventures by Disney), it's my heart saying I want to experience more adventure in my life apart from its monotony.*
>
> *Whenever I talk about being a monk, it's my heart saying I want to deepen my relationship with God apart from the distractions of this world.*
>
> *And whenever I suggest going to lunch with you, planning a*

trip to Lake Arrowhead, or asking, "What do you want to do today?" it's my heart saying I want to spend more time with just you.

I still desire you as much as when my eyes caught their first glimpse of you from the bandstand.

—Hugh

These few sentences of his, so aptly worded, cleared up years of misunderstanding. But then, my love language is words of affirmation. I live for explanations in which he says, "I didn't mean to hurt you. I just meant...."

I found Hugh's explanation of how to read between the lines so helpful and healing that I asked him to provide more insight on what men typically mean when they throw out a statement that sounds startling to their wives.

This is what Hugh had to offer.

"Don't Skip the Small Print"

Hugh McMenamin

Ladies, don't skip "the small print." What I mean by that is "learn to read between the lines"...or rather *his* lines. A man will at times make statements that sound startling or confusing to his wife:

- I hate my job.
- Ever thought about moving?
- How'd you like to go to Tahiti?
- Living in the country sounds nice.
- I want to make some changes around here.
- I've thought about looking for different work.

These statements might even sound negative, like he's

dumping or venting or having a midlife crisis. What tends to happen next is his wife has an equally startling response (most of the time it's something she just thinks in her head, but sometimes she might even say it aloud):

- Here we go again.
- He's found someone else.
- He knows we can't afford that.
- He wishes he had a different life from the one he has with me. He wants a divorce!
- He's unhappy with me.
- He will never be content with what he has.

Yet between those lines is what her man means or is trying to say:

- I'm reevaluating my career goals. I believe I can do more or better in life.
- I'd like more adventure in our life.
- I need more spontaneity in life.
- I miss a simpler life with less pressures and demands.
- I'd like to make more money to be a better provider.
- I might be running out of time to complete some long-awaited dreams.

Scripture says, "The plans in the heart of a man is like deep water, but a man [or woman] of understanding draws it out" (Proverbs 20:5 NASB). By being a woman of understanding and insight, you can draw your husband's dreams out of him by taking the time to listen for what is not being said and then asking questions about the stirring that is going on below the surface. Ask him some questions like, "You're thinking about something, aren't you? What is it?" and "That's interesting. Tell me more about what is on your heart and mind." And if you really want to dip deep into

> that well, try asking, "How can I support you in whatever is on your mind and heart right now?" When he knows you are listening and really seeking to understand him, he will make the effort to explain or dream aloud—and then you have truly entered the sacred ground of a man's heart.

When he knows you are listening and really seeking to understand him, he will make the effort to explain or dream aloud.

Hugh's insights lead me to believe we can close the gap from misunderstandings, assumptions, and even offenses by taking the time to listen to our husbands so they open their hearts further.

Closing the Gap

I asked some wives whom I respect to give me advice on how they close the gap in their marriage and prevent their husbands from becoming distant. In some cases, I asked their husbands the same questions. This is what they offered:

- *Respect and yield to his lead.* Chris, who has been married to Dan for nearly 30 years, said, "Keeping my husband from becoming distant at times is still a work in progress, yet yielding to his leading, keeping the confrontations to a minimum, and more sex pretty much guarantee him not being distant."
- *Refrain from negative responses.* Debbie said, "I've learned that I need to become a safe place for my husband to share his heart. What I mean is that I need to refrain from rolling my eyes, criticizing his ideas, or throwing a sarcastic barb when he's talking!" As we let our husbands know that

we will listen nonjudgmentally, we may find they open their hearts more readily and their mouths more often.

- *Reconnect regularly.* Debbie added that she and her husband have a regular gap-closing routine. "We are absolutely committed to date nights once a week. We are vigilant about protecting that time! During those date nights, we talk a lot about all sorts of things, and I try to be a good listener, especially when he talks about his hopes and ideas."

  Tyler said his wife Connie helps close the gap that tends to develop between the two of them when she shows him she is genuinely interested in things that happened in his day. "When we do a physical activity together (anything shoulder to shoulder) that helps us reconnect. Also, when she tells me she's feeling distant or that we need to do something together that's different from what we've been doing, that helps me see that she's attempting to close the gap."

- *Realize it may take that "extra step."* My cousin, Lisa, whom I introduced in chapter 3, said she and her husband, Jason, learned how to communicate with one another when they started attending, and eventually leading, a couples small group at church. "As good as I thought we had become at communicating, I realized that we'd only begun to scratch the surface when we started leading a couples small group," Lisa said. "I can't tell you how many times the men discussed how they would view a conversation or phrase and the women heard something totally different. It was an eye-opening experience. I realized communication isn't a one and done, confess it all and you're forever good to go. It takes work, and it takes more than just a lot of words. It takes commitment to go the step further of getting into a good couples group to allow you to think outside of your normal way of communicating."

- *Remain open to each other.* Connie believes she and Tyler are able to stay connected and on the same page "by keeping our hearts open to one another, in the Lord. We can spend time together, we can 'pray together' (I can listen to Tyler pray for us and stay quiet), but when I am holding back, which is something I realized recently that I was doing, I feel our relationship weaken. I start to feel disconnected and alone. Even when I spend time with the Lord as well as my husband, but have my heart turned from him or closed off, it's like I'm shutting down valves that the main pump is trying to pump the relationship out to. I'm not allowing it to reach me completely. As soon as I started to literally turn toward my husband during our time together, facing him—and then not just waiting for him to speak, but sharing my own heart and sharing my own prayer when he was done—I felt connected immediately. The kink in our relationship hose had been removed, and I felt the burst of everything God was trying to pour into me, through my husband."

- *Remind him how important he is to you.* Connie said, "I speak up and remind Tyler how important it is to me that we stay connected. I let him know I don't want to just walk through the days side by side, I want quality. I don't wait for it to happen."

Start Expressing Your Heart

Tara, 34, has been married to Chris for ten years. They have children and lead busy lives and found themselves in a place where she was concerned about their ability to communicate with one another. So she did something creative that eliminated the gap and enabled her and her husband to start reconnecting daily. I'll let her tell you the story:

"Chris has a very chill personality; I do as well. Communication is something I would say we don't do the best. One night I was kind of at a loss for how I could reignite the spark between us. It seemed like we had been going in circles for so long and nothing worked. So, after praying, I just felt led to write something to him in my journal. I left it out for him, and he responded by writing back to me in the journal. In fact, he responded to it so well that it's just become an everyday thing.

"Chris and I now journal to each other every day. We leave a journal in the bathroom, and we each write a note to the other in it every day. Something silly, loving, a concern, prayers, or praises. This has become something I'm eager to read each morning. It opens him up to communicate better.

"It was easy to start. I just had an empty journal, and I remembered Chris isn't the best verbal communicator but is awesome with writing (he always writes me the best cards). So I figured the journal would be a less threatening way for him to express himself. It worked!

"I love the most when he has written, 'Thank you for building me up.' To know he appreciates me encouraging his walk with the Lord... Well, a wife doesn't need much more than that!

"After trying so many ways to get what I need from my husband, the journal has been my most successful attempt. It is truly one of the greatest gifts we both get from each other every day. Plus, it's something we can hold on to forever. It really has drawn us closer."

WORKING IT THROUGH

Can you try something like what Tara did with the journal to draw your husband's heart closer to yours and begin to close that gap?

"Don't sit back and wait for it to happen," said Connie. "Don't expect your husband to read your mind. If you want to trust more, be trustworthy; if you feel like you're not being understood, quiet yourself and sit back and listen to your husband the way you'd like him to listen and understand you. Do you long for more passion? Set up a time for you to have a day together where you can talk, listen, and do an activity together and allow that time to lead you both to a deeper level of intimacy, which will give you a desire for passion. Finally, submit to God. Pray and ask the Lord for a stronger desire for your husband, ears to hear him, and opportunities to trust and submit to his leadership."

PRAYING IT THROUGH

If you're ready to close that gap and experience more communication with your husband, pray this prayer with me:

> *Lord, thank You that You know every detail of my relationship with my husband. And You know exactly what it will take to close the gap that has begun to widen, or to prevent the gap from developing in the first place. Help me be sensitive to Your Holy Spirit and know when to speak and when to be silent, when to pray for him and when to encourage, when to reach out and touch him and when to allow him his space. As You have extended love toward me, help me to willingly extend love and understanding to him. In Jesus' name, amen.*

YOUR FOCUS FOR THE WEEK

Start the "journal adventure" with your husband. Write something positive to or about him in a blank book or journal and leave it open so he can see it. You may find your husband feels it's much safer to write out what he feels or thinks rather than to say it and risk it coming out wrong. If he responds, make sure you reinforce to him how much you appreciate his words and then find ways to reward him for communicating with you in that manner. See how long the two of you can keep that journal going back and forth, but make sure you don't put pressure on him to participate. Make it something fun that he looks forward to reading, even if it's just you writing to him for a while. When he's ready, he'll respond.

9

Help Him Out

Becoming His Reliable Partner

The LORD God said, "It is not good for the man to be alone. I will make a helper suitable for him."

GENESIS 2:18

Not long ago I received this e-mail from a middle-aged man asking for help:

> I've been married 16 years. I never thought this would happen, but I've become very attracted to a woman I work with. She isn't younger or thinner or even prettier than my wife. But she's someone who lights up when I walk into the room, the way my wife once did. She helps me enthusiastically with whatever I need at work, and I really enjoy working with her. I know I shouldn't be attracted to her and shouldn't look forward to seeing her every day. Please help. How do I start feeling that same way toward my wife again? What can I do so my wife will want to be around me as much as this woman at work does?

I hate getting letters like that. And I get far too many of them. I hate receiving them because there are no simple answers to a situation like that. And I always wish the wife had contacted me to say, "I've lost interest in my husband, but I'd like to get that spark back. What can I do?" because that might be a better scenario to work with. Most of the time in situations like this the wife is oblivious. Why shouldn't she be? He committed to her. They're married. She's probably busy because she's caring for their kids and trying to keep their home together in addition to working a job to help them keep the house.

I really wanted to respond by saying, "Don't be so stupid! Change jobs if you have to! Your marriage is more important than how this woman makes you *feel*."

But he was asking for *help*. And I figured I might only have one shot at it.

I responded to his e-mail, suggesting he communicate gently to his wife how very much he loves her and wants to feel connected with her and ask her if they can seriously think about the things they can do to reconnect—share a project together, plan a trip together, commit to weekly date nights, and so on. (I also suggested he seek a job change so he was not in the presence of the other woman, thereby protecting him from temptation and ultimately protecting his marriage.) I instructed him to start praying about how he can communicate this situation to his wife, even letting her know he's willing to change jobs in order to save his marriage. (That speaks volumes to a wife about how important a man's marriage is to him.) All in all, I laid the burden on *him* to reconnect with his wife.

I never heard back from him to find out if he had talked to his wife or if he stayed in that tempting situation at work because it *felt* better and fed his ego. But I did file that e-mail away in my mind as a reminder of what men want. Most of the time it isn't a pretty face, a hot body, or a wild and adventurous spirit (although those three wouldn't hurt, I'm sure).

Most of the time men want a connection just like we do. They want a partnership, a teammate, a helper. Someone to enthusiastically come alongside them and make their lives brighter, better, easier. That's the way they were designed. And that's *why* we were designed.

Most of the time men want a connection just like we do. They want a partnership, a teammate, a helper.

Helper by Design

In the creation account in Genesis 1, we read that God created the light, the earth, the sky and seas, and everything in it that crawls, flies, and swims, and He saw that it was "good." God then created man in His own image and saw that it was "very good." But then in Genesis 2, we read for the first time in creation that God sees something that is *not* good:

> The LORD God said, "It is not good for the man to be alone. I will make a helper suitable for him"...for Adam no suitable helper was found. So the LORD God caused the man to fall into a deep sleep; and while he was sleeping, he took one of the man's ribs and then closed up the place with flesh. Then the LORD God made a woman from the rib he had taken out of the man, and he brought her to the man (verses 18,20-22).

Notice that God *didn't* say, "I will make a being that is lesser than him physically to cling to him." He also didn't say, "I will make an intellectually superior being to lord over him." Nor did He say, "I will make a duplicate of him that has a few different physical parts." God said, "I will make a *helper* who is *suitable for him.*" God designed a perfect *counterpart*—not a clone—to help the man work, play, think, decide, enjoy life, and grow old with. God even took the man's rib to make the woman who was designed to be, literally, at his side. God's plan was that the two work together, shoulder to shoulder, to complement one another and balance each other with their unique strengths.

God designed a perfect counterpart*—not a clone—to help the man work, play, think, decide, enjoy life, and grow old with.*

God did not create Eve to be Adam's mother or his maid. She was not made to be his supervisor or his doormat. He made Eve to ultimately be Adam's *helper*—to rule creation alongside him and to complement and complete him. (I hope you know the difference between compliment—to say nice things to him—and *complement*—to add to, enhance, improve, or make perfect.)

God's idea was that woman, His crowning act of creation, would make man's life complete. Funny how women are often the ones searching for a husband, thinking their lives won't be complete without one. But God's intention for adding woman to man's life was so *he* could be complete.

God's intention for adding woman to man's life was so he *could be complete.*

More Than a Helper

In Genesis 2:18, when God said He would make a *helper* suitable for Adam, God used the same word that describes the role and ministry of the Holy Spirit in the New Testament. The Holy Spirit is called our *helper*—and He is also our counselor, comforter, intercessor, and advocate. The Hebrew word translated *helper* in Genesis 2:18 can also be translated as one who brings unique strengths and qualities to the other; these qualities, found only in the woman, complete the union between man and woman.[1] This word is also used in the Old Testament in reference to God Himself in Psalm 54:4, where David tells us that God is our *helper.* It is a title of honor and great worth. In giving you to your husband as his *helper*, God was giving your man someone who was designed to act, in some ways, as his counselor, comforter, intercessor, and advocate.[2]

Think about the beauty of that. You were designed to be your husband's helper—both spiritually and otherwise. That means your discernment, that sixth sense you get when you feel like something is wrong but you can't put your finger on it, your caution and practical advice when it comes to finances, your conviction about something that he doesn't yet see, could all be attributed to the way you were wired by God to be your husband's helper.

Be his God-appointed helper with the finances (if that's your strong point), with the kids, with his goals, with his health—not like a mother who hovers, but like a companion who covers. You can cover him with your discernment, your prayers, your care, and your love.

Be His Teammate

Now, I've heard wives say, "My husband doesn't want my help. He would prefer to do things himself." I imagine that might be the case in some situations. My husband has never been the kind who wanted to be waited upon—even when he is sick. Sometimes when I offer to help him in the kitchen he assures me he has it under control. When he's working on a project, I might walk in and ask, "How can I help?" and he will say, "I've got this." Sometimes it feels like he doesn't want me in the room. But his intention is to spare me the frustration he's feeling when a project is taking a while to complete or not coming together correctly. Or he simply doesn't *need* help. However, when it's done, he sometimes asks two or three times if I like it. I can tell that, like any man, he appreciates the praise upon completion, but sometimes not necessarily the help during the project. Yet every man wants a teammate at some point in the process. Ask yours how you can be a part of his team, even if it's just bringing him something cold to drink, though you know you are capable of more.

Offer Him "Wife Support"

I asked Hugh to offer some insight on how men most want help from their wives. Having ministered to men for nearly 30 years—including leading small-group sessions where men talked about their innermost desires when it came to life, their wives, and their life's goals—Hugh offered this:

"Husbands want 'wife support' just like someone who is having difficulty breathing needs 'life support.'"

"Husbands want 'wife support' just like someone who is having difficulty breathing needs 'life support.'"

Hugh said one of the ways a wife can show support to her husband and truly help him out is to trust him when he wants to take a risk.

"When he says, 'Let's do this' and you haven't had time to calculate the risks, costs, and other factors, realize he desires to live spontaneously and adventurously.

"When he says, 'Trust me on this one,' he might not have all the details, he might not be able to explain why he wants to do something, but trust him anyway. Women call it a *sixth sense*, but men call it a *gut feeling*. If he says, 'I'm going with my gut,' indulge him. Trust his male instinct at times. By doing that, you are helping him out."

I'll admit this is a difficult one for me. If his "risk" doesn't represent financial wisdom or seem like a good idea for good, tangible reasons, it may be a situation in which you need to pray, seek God's guidance, and then proceed carefully or talk with him about what you are sensing as his "Holy Spirit helper." (I will address this more in the next chapter.)

Emily said when she trusted her husband with what looked spontaneous but scary, she learned a lot about how dependable her husband was and it greatly improved their relationship.

"George and I traveled to Ireland for three weeks as one of our last vacations before having kids," she said. "This was going to be a different type of vacation for us, as we usually did resort-type/cruise vacations. This time George wanted to bring out my adventurous side with a trip to Ireland. He had a lot of experience traveling in Europe and enjoys spontaneous traveling. I am not a spontaneous person and prefer to have everything planned out. Our previous vacations had always been planned before we departed. This time we just had our flights booked and the first couple of nights booked in Dublin when we arrived. The rest of the time was open to whatever we wanted to do. We could spend seven days in a city we enjoyed, or visit multiple cities over several days if we wanted to experience more of Ireland.

"I was extremely nervous to do this, especially since neither one of us had been to Ireland before. Yet I had to trust my husband that he would not leave me sleeping on a park bench because we couldn't find a hotel for the night. I had confidence in him and in his abilities with traveling. The trip was super successful, and the spontaneity added to our experience. I was the driver for the entire trip (my husband had to trust me to drive safely on the opposite side of the road—and those roads are *very* narrow), and I also had to trust his navigation skills for the 2,000 km we drove during the three weeks. We got lost one time, on the return trip to the airport to go home. I was freaking out that we wouldn't make it to our flight in time, yet we figured it out and made it home as planned. It all worked out, and we consider it one of our 'great adventures.'"

Ways You Can Help

I asked several wives I know how they help their husbands, and I also asked a few husbands to chime in on how they are best helped by their wives. This is the advice they offered:

Help According to Your Strengths

Emily said she has learned to help George with their two young children by looking at their strengths and doing what each does best.

"Although we are extremely different in many areas, George and I know that our differences ultimately make us stronger as a couple. We try to make our differences work *for* us to strengthen our marriage. We see this especially in raising our kids. I am a teacher, and I spend time working with our son, Max, on his letters and numbers, whereas George works with his hands and helps him builds things. He takes Max outside and teaches him the names of tools and how to use them correctly and safely. My instinct is not to dig outside with my son, and George would never think to buy ABC flashcards. Yet we both bring these very different skills to parenting and it works."

Anticipate His Needs

Helping her husband is not just about seeing to it that the children have what they need. Emily also makes sure she is helping her husband personally, by anticipating his needs and coming through for him.

"My husband is a very simple, practical man," she said. "The little things are what he values. He feels loved through my acts of service, especially when I do the dishes and his laundry. If he comes home and these things aren't done, he feels stress that he'll need to find time to do them. Yet if these chores are completed when he comes home from work, he feels loved. I don't always have a clean kitchen, but when I have done the simple act of cleaning up before he gets home, I know I am showing love by helping my husband."

Be His "Protection"

I remember seeing a James Bond movie with my husband shortly after we were married. Bond was attracted to another spy he was working with, and in one scene they were at a casino and her undercover identity was as his "executive secretary" (complete with a thigh holster for her gun underneath her sexy evening gown). I remember thinking, *That's so cool.* I often think of that visual. I want to be my husband's "executive secretary"—assisting him with what he needs while looking hot next to him (minus the gun strapped to my inner thigh, of course).

Our help can often be a form of protection.

Steve said his wife, Sophie, "will help me smooth over awkward conversations at a party by interjecting something in the conversation that makes me look good. She also works toward the good of our team by doing what's best for the family, putting her immediate dissatisfaction with me aside if we've had a conflict."

While Steve is busy at his high-stress job for a television studio, his wife, who is also busy as a choreographer and owner of her own dance school, still manages their social calendar (See? Executive secretary!) and is the one who makes sure the two of them spend time together regularly.

"She also suggests fun activities for the family and makes time in her schedule for us to have dates," Steve said.

Help Him Date You

If you and your husband don't ever "date" because you are waiting on his suggestion or initiation, give that up. *You* be the one who initiates. Yeah, in a perfect world your husband would do that and thereby make you feel cherished. But you are his helper. And one way you can help him is to schedule activities that the two of you would enjoy and that he most likely wants to do but hasn't gotten around to planning yet.

Although he gives lots of ideas and suggestions, I can't remember the last time Hugh planned one of our family vacations or personal getaways. Wait...did he ever? But, oh, that's right, there's a reason for that. I know exactly where we are with the finances. I also get a little nervous when we do something we haven't prepared for financially or can't really afford. I'm not a "do it now, pay for it later" person at all when it comes to vacations, or anything else for that matter. I'd much rather save up for it and then enjoy it, without concern for what it costs. Therefore, Hugh helps ease my mind by letting me do the planning of activities that are within our budget that we would both enjoy, and I help him by putting aside the money in the budget, getting it scheduled on the calendar, and making sure it actually happens.

Practice Random Acts of Kindness

Debbie, a busy wife who works long hours, said when she helps her husband, it pulls them closer together.

"I believe the secret to our strength as a couple is truly living out Philippians 2:4—'Do not merely look out for your own personal interests, but also for the interests of others' (NASB)—where we both strive to consider each other's interest, not just our own! So I intentionally go out of my way to help my husband, encourage my husband, and do little random acts of kindness every day. He does the same for me.

"For example, when I can see my husband is getting frustrated with a computer project, I drop what I'm doing and assist him. When I notice that he's feeling a bit discouraged, I drop what I'm doing and sit down with him to listen to what has happened during his day, and then I remind him of all the good qualities I see in him. When he fasts on

Tuesdays (in preparation for evening ministry), I make him his favorite food, so that when he comes home late that night, he'll be treated to a terrific meal."

Debbie said helping her husband like that also encourages him to help her as well.

"My husband also strives to consider *my* interests, not just his own. For instance, he knows I struggle with our sex life due to years of sexual abuse as a child, so he never pressures me to have sex and waits so patiently for me to initiate when I'm ready. What a gift! And whether my husband is tired or even upset with me, he *always* gives me a little foot massage as I'm going to bed each night. *Every* night, with no expectations. Now, that is living out Philippians 2:4!"

That verse in context reads like this:

> Do nothing from selfishness or empty conceit, but with humility of mind regard one another as more important than yourselves; do not merely look out for your own personal interests, but also for the interests of others (Philippians 2:3-4 NASB).

When you are looking out for your husband's needs more than your own, you are practicing the Bible's definition of dying to self. You are practicing Jesus' command to love sacrificially to the point of picking up your cross. And through obedience comes joy—every time.

When you are looking out for your husband's needs more than your own, you are practicing the Bible's definition of dying to self.

PRAYING IT THROUGH

Lord, thank You that You are the ultimate Helper. You, at times, move heaven and earth to come through for me. Please give me that kind of willingness and dedication to help my husband with what he needs as well. Help me anticipate his needs, help him according to my strengths, and live out Your intended role for me to be his counselor, comforter, intercessor, and friend. Help me to be sensitive to the Holy Spirit's direction so I can gently steer him toward Your will. Help me trust his lead, protect his name, and show him random acts of kindness so that he will find that he not only has a helper, but a godly guide and best friend as well. In the name of the Lord Jesus—who helps, strengthens, and empowers, amen.

YOUR FOCUS FOR THE WEEK

Memorize Philippians 2:3-4: "Do nothing out of selfish ambition or vain conceit. Rather, in humility value others above yourselves, not looking to your own interests but each of you to the interests of the others."

10

Wait It Out

Praying It Through When You'd Rather Talk It Out

Teach me, and I will be quiet;
show me where I have been wrong.

Job 6:24

I was concerned that Hugh and I were about to make a huge mistake.

Some friends of ours from church had offered to give our daughter, who had just received her driver's license, their old car. It was a Saturn wagon that they admitted was in need of some work. Dana was excited at the prospect of having a car of her own. And my husband was thrilled that our friends were willing to *give* it to us. But I had a bad feeling about it. And I couldn't shake it off.

Hugh took the car to a mechanic friend of ours at church to determine how much work needed to be done and how much money we would have to invest in it if we accepted the car from our friends. At dinner the next evening, Hugh pulled out the list (more like a novel!) of everything that our mechanic friend said needed to be repaired or replaced on the car. The bottom line was that he would only charge us for the parts, not any of the labor, but it was still going to cost us more than $2,000!

"That's not much for a car she will be able to drive," Hugh said optimistically. But still, my heart (not just the cheapskate in me) and my mind (that *might* have been the cheapskate part) told me we should steer clear of the car. "That's not a good investment," I responded. "Let's just wait."

Hugh was not at all happy. I could tell he was thinking I was being controlling and unyielding to his lead.

"Let's please give it another day or two before we decide whether to take the car," I pleaded.

Hugh's look told me he was upset that I was being difficult.

So I prayed. *Hard.*

God, only You know what's around the corner with this car. So, will You please either give us complete peace about accepting this car from our friends and paying that much money to get it fixed or provide another alternative soon? Please, God, just don't let us make a big financial mistake that we might end up regretting for years.

There seemed to be silence on God's part. But still, there was no peace. So two days later I told Hugh, "I just don't feel good about it. Please trust *me.* I really think God might have something better down the road if we just wait."

Hugh still wasn't happy. He insisted I had to be the one to tell our mechanic friend we would not be accepting his generous offer, which I did. I also told our friends that we appreciated their offer too, but didn't believe we could afford to make the necessary repairs. They understood and were fine with it.

Three days later—did you catch that? *Three days* later—a senior shut-in who wasn't able to attend our church any longer called Hugh, her longtime pastor who had been visiting her weekly, and offered us her van—a 1992 Toyota Previa that was in "fine" condition. Granted, it was 17 years old at the time—the same age as our daughter, in fact—but we figured a van that was her birth year would be not only a good, safe one but would also be a very good deal when it came to the insurance. (There's the cheapskate in me again.) We accepted her offer and took the van, and it became Dana's first vehicle.

Despite Dana's whining and complaining that she looked like an "old grandma" driving around an old van, it met her driving needs for three years. Until our friends—the same ones who had offered us their Saturn clunker three years earlier—literally begged us to let them trade their like-new sporty Saturn Vue for that now 20-year-old van! They were a family of five by then and couldn't afford a new van and thought the easiest solution would be to trade their newer car for our older van. Hugh pointed out to them that we would be getting a far better deal, but they were determined to have a used van to accommodate their growing family. So, yep, Dana got a 3-year-old Saturn Vue Hybrid (did I mention it was a hybrid too?) in exchange for that nearly 20-year-old van!

God knew what was three years around the corner when we were originally offered that Saturn clunker—a like-new Saturn Vue Hybrid—which became the best car our daughter (and her parents) has ever driven! Had I failed to wait it out and pray it through—and tell my husband I believed God had something better—we would've missed God's best for our family when it came to accepting a free car for Dana.

The Beauty of Waiting

I realize I could have talked my husband to death by recounting every reason we shouldn't take that clunker when it was offered to us. I could've also gone out and found a car myself and insisted that was a better deal. But there's something beautiful that happens when we talk to God about it and then wait it out: We end up giving God a chance to change our husbands' hearts, convince us of the direction we should go, or come through for us in a far better way than we could have ourselves.

How many times have you insisted on *talking it out* with your husband when you really should've *waited it out* to see how God could have *worked it out*? Maybe you'll never know at this point. But it may be worth a try so that you can experience more with your husband—more of what God may want to do in your life or provide on your behalf.

How many times have you insisted on talking it out *with your husband when you really should've* waited it out *to see how God could have* worked it out?

Waiting, watching, and praying when you and your husband don't agree, or during the silence on your husband's part, or when either or both of you are faced with a decision and you're not sure what to do, can give you insights into your husband's heart, God's will, and your next move. Trust me on this one. I've seen it work not only in my own marriage but among countless other couples.

Wait? Now?

I know what you're thinking. You aren't used to having to wait for anything. So why wait when it comes to talking something through with your husband?

We live in a society that doesn't know *how* to wait. We have just about everything we want *right now*. First it was fast food, then it was drive-thrus, and now it's mobile order. Our mentality is the quicker, the better. But it's not just food. We have access to Snapchat, instant chat, instant message, Instagram, air drop, real-time, live stream, and the list goes on. Unfortunately, the instant communication methods make us think that we can do personally what we can accomplish electronically, and that leads to unrealistic expectations for instant communication, instant connection, instant understanding, instant agreement, instant apologies, instant resolutions, instant trust, instant change, and instant transformation. But life doesn't work that way. Great results often take time. And some of the best things in life are worth waiting for. There's a reason trust deepens after decades of marriage rather than days. And sometimes the best things in marriage—great communication, great connection, and great relationship—come after waiting it out.

In our instant communication age, men like my husband (and possibly yours) who think internally, rather than verbally, face instant pressure to have to say or grasp or decide or commit, rather than giving it time. And we wives get frustrated by their inability to immediately read our minds, discern our thoughts, and give us instant words to comfort us or lessen our stress in the moment.

I want to offer you something that will help you experience more quality conversation and trust with your husband. I want to offer you the suggestion to *wait it out*. Wait till he understands, wait till his heart changes, wait till he agrees with you, wait till the time is right. I know, waiting is difficult. But the easiest way to wait it out is to *pray it through.*

The easiest way to wait it out is to pray it through.

When They Didn't Wait

In chapter 8 we looked at how two women in the Bible—Rachel and Michal—created a gap between themselves and their husbands when they demanded and accused rather than communicated effectively. We looked at how their situations might have fared better if they had talked lovingly with their husbands about their concerns, rather than emotionally blurting out what they were feeling. Now I want to suggest what might have happened if they had simply gone to God first and prayed it through before they spoke a word to their husbands.

Remember how Rachel was upset at not being able to have children? She was also jealous of her sister, who was able to get pregnant so easily. But had she poured out her heart to God first, I'm certain she would've had the peace that He was in control of her situation. I think prayer would have also given her the hope that her Yahweh God was the giver of every good and perfect gift. Perhaps that would have prevented her from taking matters into her own hands and giving her maid to Jacob so she could have children through her, and pursuing a competition with her sister (and eventually her sister's maid) to see who could have more babies. When we take our hearts to God, He hears. When we surrender to His will and timing, we receive peace. When we choose to do things His way we are blessed.

And if Michal—who was upset at seeing her husband, David, display himself as he danced before the ark—had come to God in prayer before talking with David, it's likely that just praying and being in God's presence would have calmed her heart and given her a softer spirit and gentler tone when she talked to her husband. Perhaps she would have refrained altogether from accusing and insulting her king/husband. Or maybe she wouldn't have felt the need to bring up the matter in the first place. When we go to God in prayer, He not only calms our hearts and gives us peace (Philippians 4:6-7), but His Spirit gives us insight and often a different perspective—*God's* perspective, not ours.

When we take our hurts, frustrations, and even anger to God, before we take them to anyone else (especially our husbands), we are able to filter our words and balance our raw emotions so we can have a more mature (and less reactionary) discussion with someone. Can you imagine how helpful that can be in marriage? God can handle your unfiltered emotions, raw language, and even your dramatics. Our husbands often can't. Prayer calms our hearts and helps us seek God's response to a situation, rather than lashing out with our own. God can temper that talk we believe we need to have. He can soften that accusation. He can pave the way for our suggestion, and He can prepare our husbands' hearts for our new approach.

Why Wait?

In addition to wanting God's blessing on every conversation you have with your husband, here are three more reasons to wait it out and pray it through instead of pushing it through when you feel you need to talk:

To gain discernment. Remember that principle from the previous chapter that you are your husband's helper and therefore you can minister to him with discernment as the Holy Spirit does? If you are going to be able to offer the wisdom and discernment of the Holy Spirit and take on the role of a godly counselor in your husband's life, you absolutely need to wait on God for how to do that rather than trying to offer wisdom and guidance on your own, which could be disastrous.

To get the right results. There have been times I have been wounded during a conversation with Hugh and times I have been hurt because I insisted that he respond a certain way and he never did. As I have learned to go to God first, He has a wonderful way of either comforting my heart and convincing me it wasn't as big of a deal as I thought it was, or softening Hugh's heart and causing him to come around and talk about it and say the healing words I needed to hear. God worked it out when I waited and prayed—not when I rushed ahead with my own agenda or insisted Hugh and I talk it through.

To give him time. Sometimes it helps to wait it out simply because your husband may need more time to process and respond than you do. Tara, who implemented the "daily journal writing" with her husband, Chris (in chapter 8), said, "After voicing my concerns to my husband about something, instead of expecting a reaction from him right away, I give him a day or so to respond. Chris is an inward thinker; I am an outward thinker. Knowing that really has strengthened our way of communicating."

Trust the Timing

It used to be very difficult to wait for what seemed like days for Hugh to process something and then respond. But while I was waiting it out—and praying it through—God's Holy Spirit revealed something to me about my husband's heart and his way of processing life. During that long day or two when I'm trying to get a response out of him, he is thinking about the best way to express himself, the best choice of words, the most effective approach, the most conducive tone, and the timing in which to bring it up again. Oh, how I wish I could say I spend that much time and mental energy before I address an important topic with him. How much more graceful *and godly* my words would be if I practiced that approach.

That realization caused me to thank God for my husband rather than complain that he doesn't process things quickly (and perhaps less carefully) than I do. That can be a blessing, girls, to have a husband who doesn't shoot from the hip and say whatever is on his mind, no matter how rudely or harshly it comes across. When your husband is an internal processor, there are likely less hurtful words spoken and more careful words chosen.

When your husband is an internal processor,
there are likely less hurtful words spoken
and more careful words chosen.

Waiting it out also gives us a chance to hear from the Holy Spirit about our own attitudes and actions. Barbara, my friend and longtime spiritual mentor, whom I introduced in chapter 6, offered this:

"The minute the Holy Spirit nudges my spirit that I have said something ugly, or said something in a short, maternal, bossy, or impatient manner, I immediately—or as soon as it is appropriate—own up to the rude behavior. And that doesn't mean I initiate that by saying, 'I need to speak with you about something' or 'Can we talk?' I think those phrases make a guy's stomach turn into knots. Instead, I say, 'I need to clear the air…' or 'Let me take a minute and apologize for…' or 'I'm sorry for…'"

Learn to Read Him

Emily knows the art of waiting it out when it comes to her husband, who is also an internal processor.

"Although George is extremely quiet about his feelings and emotions, I've learned how to 'read' him now that we've been married seven years. Early on in our marriage, I wanted to talk things out right away if I sensed that something was wrong. This was the wrong approach, I learned! George doesn't always know what he is feeling right away and needs time to think his emotions through (hard for me to understand, since I'm very in tune with my emotions). I have learned to give George a lot of time, and I let him come to me with the conversation. When he is ready, he will share what is on his mind and how he's feeling and then we can talk it through. This has been very helpful in the last couple of years because it makes for a much more productive conversation when we are both open to talking. I like to fix the problems right away, but I've learned that is counterproductive and will only lead to more stress for George."

Pray with Him

I'm sure you've heard this advice as often as I have:

The couple that prays together stays together.

It's hard to be angry with your husband when you're praying with and for him.

There's not a problem with you and your spouse that God can't handle through prayer.

I'll be the first to tell you, praying *with* your husband is easier said than done.

When I'm with my godly girlfriends and we decide to pray about something, we just launch in. And it feels so natural. Why, though, is it so difficult to pray with our husbands? If you hit the same obstacles we do, see "How to Encourage Your Husband to Pray with You" on page 205. (It's based on *When Couples Walk Together*, a book Hugh and I coauthored several years ago), which offers simple steps for you and your husband to overcome the obstacles and start praying together.

Now, if you've followed the steps from that article and your husband still won't pray *with* you, that shouldn't stop you from praying. Maybe you're married to a man who doesn't share your faith. If that's the case, don't push him to pray with you. Talk to God about him more than you talk to him about God.

Praying with your husband (if he shares your faith) is important. Chris, a longtime friend of mine, told me that praying with her husband is one of the things that has really strengthened her nearly 30-year marriage to her husband, Dan.

"We've had some challenges with our youngest son, and coming together very often in prayer for him has brought us closer to one another," Chris said. Prayer has also strengthened their relationships with their children, and has helped shape them into praying spouses and parents as well.

Although praying with your husband is important, praying *without* him is equally important and just might be more effective in certain situations, regardless of what you've been taught.

I'm sure you've heard the verse, "For where two or three gather in my name, there am I with them" (Matthew 18:20), and you believe that means if you and your husband pray together, you get more of God's ear than if you prayed by yourself, right? Not so.

That verse, in the context of Matthew 18:15-20, refers to judgment in the church. The *two or three* that are gathered together refers to two or three witnesses coming together to confront a believer in judgment, whereby God will be the judge in the midst of them. Yet that verse has been so widely taken out of context that upon hearing it, most believe it refers to the power of praying with more than one person. The problem is, if that verse were referring to prayer, then it would be implying that if you are praying by yourself, God is *not* there in your midst. And that is absolutely not true. God hears you even if you're the only one in the room.

In Psalm 139:1-4, David sang of God knowing his thoughts from afar and his words before he spoke them. God knows what each and every one of us is going to pray before we even say or pray it. So you are never unheard when it comes to prayer. Many a person throughout the Bible prayed to God all by themselves and God heard them, just as much as if they were praying in community—or among thousands.

Prayer with your husband will definitely help you feel more connected to his heart. But prayer alone with just you and God will help you feel more connected to *God's* heart. That is why both are important.

Just You and God

Here are some issues to pray about on your own, whether or not your husband is willing to pray with you.

When You Don't Agree

I shared with you a story at the beginning of this chapter about how Hugh and I didn't agree on taking the clunker car that was offered to us. And by praying it through, I was able to have the peace to wait on God to do something even better. But God has also used Hugh to hold me off when I wanted to rush into something.

Earlier this year my daughter and I got in our minds that we wanted to replace our carpet downstairs with wood laminate flooring. We believed it would be better for Hugh, who suffers allergies now and then from our beloved cat, Mowgli. We also wanted to update the look of our condo. Dana and I also looked at granite countertops to replace the old tile and grungy grout in our kitchen, but the cost was just too much and we figured we didn't truly *need* it. So we were pushing hard for the new flooring. We priced it and I told Hugh we could take the money out of savings, but he didn't feel quite right about it.

Hugh insisted that we wait. "We don't know if we might end up paying taxes this year, so let's wait until after April," he said.

"But we have the money in savings," I countered.

Hugh was insistent. "I'm just not feeling at peace about it. Please wait and please trust me on this," he said firmly. I was so convinced we should have that flooring that I whined about it to God in prayer the next morning. It was very clear what God was saying to my heart during my prayer time: *Listen to your husband. Follow his lead.*

I didn't bother arguing with God. He usually won't budge on things. So I waited it out and forgot about the flooring. Until the end of March when we discovered wet carpet from a slab leak underneath our kitchen floor and entryway. Long story short, we ended up getting all new wood flooring downstairs *and* beautiful new granite countertops at *no* expense to us. It was all paid by our insurance company in the reconstruction process after our water damage was assessed. Had I rushed ahead and not waited on Hugh and God for that flooring, we would've paid a few thousand dollars for it, only to have it all ripped up a month later and reinstalled again after the leak. By waiting when Hugh said, "Let's wait" and listening to God when He said, *Listen to your husband*, we didn't pay anything for what turned out to be a $15,000-downstairs remodel in our home.

Take it to God when you need your husband to fall in line with what you feel the Holy Spirit is prompting you to do. And take it to God when you need peace about falling in line with your husband's lead. God can accomplish far more through prayer—and your waiting—than you and your husband can through arguing.

God can accomplish far more through prayer—and your waiting—than you and your husband can through arguing.

When He Disappoints You

Ladies, telling God, *My husband disappointed me* is so much more effective than telling your husband. I'm not saying don't discuss problems. I'm saying that your husband is going to disappoint you, maybe quite often, and chances are he already knows it. By going to God with your disappointment, you are avoiding heaping guilt on your man, and you are consulting with the Holy Spirit, who can convict his heart way better than you can, without you having to say a word.

You are also praying *for* him, which softens your heart toward him and keeps you from becoming bitter. Your man may begin to avoid you if you are frequently telling him he's doing something wrong. No one wants to hear that. Especially your husband. Talk to God about your husband before talking to him. God will let you know when it's something you should just leave in His capable hands.

When You Aren't Sure How to Address a Matter

When you suspect that your husband might be hiding something, or you feel you need to confess something to him, or maybe you feel strongly about quitting your job or wanting another child, it may be difficult to know how to bring up the topic. What do you say? How do you say it? What if it doesn't come across the way you mean it to? How will you respond if he reacts a certain way? Take it to God and wait upon His direction for how and when to proceed. God has a way of going before us into uncertainty and paving the path for us by giving us wisdom and insight, directing us as to the timing, and preparing another's heart for what we are about to discuss.

PRAYING IT THROUGH

Let's take anything you are struggling with in your marriage, or anything you feel you need to talk through with your husband, and give it to God in prayer right now.

> *God, thank You for knowing all things—what is around the corner as well as what is years ahead. Help me trust in You*

with all my heart and not lean on my own understanding when it comes to issues I feel I need to talk through with my husband. In all my ways I acknowledge and submit to You, and I know You will make my paths straight (Proverbs 3:5-6) by preparing my husband's heart or preparing me to follow his lead. Lord, slow me down so I don't rush ahead of my husband or ahead of You. Soften my heart and tune my ears to hear Your voice, heed Your direction, and wait for Your timing. Give me discernment to know when to follow my husband's lead, and when to take it to You and wait for Your wisdom in how I can counsel and direct my husband in a better way. Thank You for being my Wisdom and my Strength. In Jesus' name, amen.

My friend, before I close out this chapter, let me just say that I would consider it an honor to pray for you and anything that you struggle with in your marriage. Just contact me at my website (StrengthForTheSoul.com/Contact Cindi) and write "Chapter 10—prayer request" in the subject line and I'll be happy to pray for you. I don't need the details, because God knows them. If you need to, just put this book down right now and e-mail me what's on your mind. I will take it to our heavenly Father in prayer. And I'll do my best to respond back to you with a note that I did.

YOUR FOCUS FOR THE WEEK

Schedule a time this week to pray *with* your husband (if possible), *for* your husband, and *for* your marriage. Record here when you will do that.

11

Stick It Out

Choosing Love When You'd Rather Leave

When I found the one my heart loves.
I held him and would not let him go.

Song of Songs 3:4

Because you picked up this book on how to experience more with your husband, I'm guessing you're not in the frame of mind of ever wanting to leave him.

None of us ever intends to walk away from the vows we made to each other before God and witnesses. None of us ever expects we'll be betrayed by the person who promised us forever. And we certainly never think we will fall out of love or get to the point where we just don't want to be with the person we promised our hearts to. Yet it happens. More than half of all marriages today end in divorce because one person or the other—or both—call it quits. People who were once so in love eventually choose to leave rather than stick it out.

That doesn't have to be you. As far as it depends on you, you can be a woman resolved to stick it out—for richer, for poorer, in sickness and in health, for better or for worse.

I think we all just need lifelines to hold on to when crisis hits, or the feelings fade, or we start to believe the lie that we'd be better off without our spouse.

Misty is one of those who, despite the odds, held on to her lifeline—and her husband.

This is her story.

"The day after my fifty-third birthday I asked my husband of fifteen years to meet me at home at 3:00 p.m. on an urgent matter. He knew something was wrong because I am normally working at that hour. When he arrived home, he found me sitting in our kitchen with a yellow legal pad of paper with a long vertical line drawn down the center. I asked him to provide a list of liquid assets he would require to live alone for an undetermined amount of time. To his surprise, I had three bags packed upstairs and a reservation made for an extended hotel stay, along with several furnished apartment ads. I told him I didn't want a divorce, just a separation.

"I finally had his attention.

"So how did we get here? It wasn't just one event. It was a cumulative total of arguing over dumb stuff, digging our heels in to our viewpoints, lack of thoughtful discussion, not putting the other first, and the fact that we practice our faith differently. (He is Roman Catholic and I am Protestant, which meant I was attending a Protestant church by myself.)

"My husband was a man full of pride and selfishness, and I was a woman full of resentment and anger. Our marriage started off with geographic separation due to his military career, and he wasn't completely transparent with me about some issues before we said, 'I do.'

"Over the next few years, depression and hopelessness began to slowly build up in my heart and soul, just like plaque in one's arteries. Over time this buildup became more destructive and unhealthy. I was amazed at how subtly it crept into everything I did, and I didn't realize how much damage was being done until I reached a breaking point. I was so unhappy and fed up with my husband, but I was desperate to save my marriage and not walk away.

"By the grace of God and His timing, my church was sponsoring an eight-week marriage class that was starting in two weeks. I went to my church's website and immediately signed up and paid the fee. I also discovered a link that offered a marriage mentor. I printed the four-page mentor application and filled out every line and answered some very embarrassing but necessary questions. I then prayed to God that my husband would agree to both the marriage class and the mentors—not realizing four weeks later we would be sitting in our kitchen dividing our assets. God knew things were going to get really bad even before I did. How ironic that Satan worked double time to destroy my marriage after I made the decision to do everything I could to save it. By the third week of the marriage class things were so bad at home that I had sunk to a state of hopelessness. Now add a scoop of embarrassment and a double scoop of pride: I felt ashamed to even return to the class.

"But then the breakthrough happened. Because my husband and I were in a marriage class with ten other couples and we had marriage mentors, we were surrounded with lifelines. All we had to do was reach up and grab hold of what I now see were ropes hanging from heaven. If we hadn't had the class and the mentors at the same time I was considering separation, I believe things would have turned out differently.

"My husband and I realized our marriage strength was rooted in our commitment to God, our classmates, and another couple—our marriage mentors. The marriage class is long over, but the biblical strategies we learned in that class, along with tools from marriage retreats we've attended, helped us neutralize any more buildup of resentment, pride, or selfishness."

Where Do You Stand?

Do you and your husband have several Christian couples around you who can hold you up when you start to feel you're sinking? Do you have an older, wiser, stronger couple who has been down similar roads you and your husband have traveled or who can, because of their strength as a couple, mentor you and your husband and hold you two accountable? Do you invest in marriage retreats and constantly learn ways to become stronger together? All of those resources helped Misty and her husband, and all of those things can help you and your husband as well should you ever get to the point of thinking you can't stick it out together.

Strategies for Sticking It Out

Misty said there were many strategies she and her husband learned as they encountered struggles. Most of them are based in God's Word and have become principles to live by. One of the most essential was learning how to show her husband honor and respect.

Honor and Respect Him

"Respect is so vital in a godly marriage," Misty said. She cited several passages of Scripture that she had to learn to live by when it came to relating to her husband:

- "Be devoted to one another in love. Honor one another above yourselves" (Romans 12:10).
- "Do nothing out of selfish ambition or vain conceit. Rather, in humility value others above yourselves" (Philippians 2:3).
- "Each one of you also must love his wife as he loves himself, and the wife must respect her husband" (Ephesians 5:33).

Misty said, "The reason I referenced these scriptures is because my husband said he did not feel respected by me on a consistent basis. He came to that conclusion because he said my word choices and tone of voice were condescending. That feedback really hurt, and I didn't necessarily agree with it, but I needed to hear him out.

"I took Colossians 4:6 to heart, which says, 'Let your conversation be always full of grace, seasoned with salt, so that you may know how to answer everyone.' And Ephesians 4:29 also helped me by reminding me that my speech should be 'only what is helpful for building others up.' I also had to remember that the tongue is a wicked and dangerous weapon that builds us up or tears us down (James 3:6-10). Verbal arguments are fought with our tongues (word choices) and tone!"

Misty had to be aware of what she was saying to her husband, as well as how she was saying it, through tone and body language. And a key to doing that was learning, with her husband, how to deploy "the safety valve."

Deploy the "Safety Valve"

"We were stuck in a frustrating cycle of how to resolve our differing opinions or viewpoints without arguing or disrespecting each other," Misty said. "We disagreed on everything from what size nail to use when hanging a curtain rod to how long he runs the water when washing dishes. I needed to learn how to respect him *when* I was disagreeing with him."

The solution? Misty and her husband now have what they refer to as a "safety valve" that they tap into when either one of them is feeling disrespected.

"My husband will say, 'I am feeling disrespected by you right now.' I then ask him, 'In what way?' This dialogue and exchange tells both of us we are heading toward a verbal conflict and we need to rephrase or tone down our position. The key is to deploy the safety valve strategy immediately before getting too deep in the conflict.

Deploy the safety valve strategy immediately.

"We learned that if we waited too long, the verbal argument would quickly escalate and the more emotionally invested we became—hence more fuel for the fire! We are both very competitive people, and one of us always had to 'win' the argument. We're thankful we figured this one out because we didn't want our marriage to turn into a 'pay and owe' sheet where we were keeping tabs on how many victories or losses we scored.

"Because my husband is created in God's image, if I respect God, I need to respect my husband."

The key, she said, was figuring out how to disagree with him on his viewpoints but maintain an attitude of respect.

"Sarcasm and rolling my eyes always got me in trouble!" she admitted. "Our marriage experienced a huge growth spurt when we figured out how to respect each other when we disagreed on things. I think both of us needed to learn that disagreement doesn't equal disrespect.

Once we defined both of these areas, we were able to move forward into a healthier and happier relationship. We are able to have 'safe' conversations that allow both of us to express personal feelings or opinions."

Fight Fair

Another strategy Misty and her husband learned was how to fight fair.

"One of the best takeaways my husband and I learned from a marriage retreat we attended was a strategy on how to fight fair. I thought this session was rather odd—a Christian marriage therapist was teaching 150 Christian couples how to have a verbal argument in a fair and safe way. The speaker gave all of us a phrase to invoke when we felt an argument was brewing. One half of the couple was supposed to shout out the letters *DA*, which stood for 'dumb argument.' Upon hearing the letters *DA*, both parties must immediately stop arguing and let it go. When I heard this tactic I laughed out loud because it sounded so ridiculous in its simplicity. The truth of the matter is it actually works! My husband and I learned this four years ago, and we still use it today."

Forgive and Restart

We looked in chapter 4 at the importance of forgiveness. But I believe it's significant that this is one of the strategies Misty had to learn and practice in order to stick it out in her marriage.

"The turning point for me that allowed me to gain more trust, passion, understanding, and respect for my husband was when he publicly admitted to our fellow marriage class students (about 20 people) that he was not as transparent as he should have been when he asked for my hand in marriage. For nearly 15 years I had been harboring resentment toward my husband because he was not completely truthful about his life when he was dating me. He had left out some details that may have changed my answer when he asked me to marry him—one of which was that he was deeply committed to a very structured form of religion. My husband was a bit of a religious chameleon and seemed to enjoy my church and worship style while we were dating. But after we married, he quickly reverted to the religion of his roots. There were also other personal topics and areas of instability I would have appreciated knowing more about before we entered into our marriage contract.

"Fifteen years later, after my husband and I stood hand in hand in front of 20 of our marriage classmates, where he publicly admitted and apologized for his lack of full disclosure before we were married, I forgave him. My forgiveness was instantaneous. Tears were streaming down my face, and I was crying so hard that I had to turn my back to the audience to regain my composure. I was so proud of my husband and so grateful that God could melt my hard heart. The words my husband spoke were exactly what I needed to hear in order to finally bury my bitterness. This was such a profound and miraculous moment that we decided to start our marriage over. Using today's vernacular, we rebooted our marriage and now consider ourselves married only a few months!"

How can a couple married 15 years now see themselves as newlyweds? Crisis has a way of pulling a couple tighter together. Because they chose to stick it out, Misty and her husband are now stronger than ever.

Through Whatever May Come

Barbara, whose story we looked at in chapter 6, remembers the day her husband, Don, walked through the door with disturbing news. Don, a pastor, had been "reassigned" and did not feel the assignment was coming from God.

"It was something we didn't want to do," Barbara said. "We knew it wasn't for us, it was not our calling, and we believed we were being set aside by dysfunctional leadership.

"When my husband asked the senior pastor, 'What if I don't see this as God's next step for me?' he was told, 'Then we'll help you leave.' So that night both of us had numerous reasons why we could and should leave. But we had to ask ourselves, would that choice to leave on our own be surrendering to God, who was sovereign over the decision for us to move to another ministry?

"The next morning my husband was lying on the bed staring off into the distance, and I walked back into the room in my bathrobe—neither of us having spoken that morning—and I said, 'When you met me, you couldn't believe God had set each of us aside to serve Him together. And when I met you, I never dreamed there was a man out there for me. So we have to take the assignment because we can't miss whatever it is God is trying to show or teach us through all of this.' We both had tears in our eyes as I said that.

"It was almost three years in 'Joseph's jail' before we were released from that reassigned position. I would add that, like Joseph, we were not immediately restored; but we are still walking together, trusting and believing—all the while comforting and encouraging each other during both the up days and the down days.

"It appears that trust, passion, and understanding are forged in adversity," Barbara said. "Maybe *battle* is a better word."

Suit Up for Battle

I'm sure none of us thought of *battle* when we stood at the altar on our wedding day and promised each other "I do." We thought of love, happiness, and a promising future of sunshine and blue skies. But *battle*? And yet marriage *is* a battle when we are determined to stick it out for the sake of our commitment to God and to one another. We must *fight* for our marriage at times. Fight the enemy of our soul. Fight the temptation of our flesh. Fight the stubbornness of our pride. And fight through the hard times together.

God's Word offers us battle gear for this fight. Ephesians 6 refers to it as "God's armor" and provides instructions in how to suit up and stand firm.

Here is how Scripture instructs us to do battle (with some parenthetical additions of mine to help you apply these battle instructions to your marriage). As you read these instructions, think about your marriage and the attempts of the Enemy to take us down, take us out, or make one of us walk away:

> A final word: Be strong in the Lord and in his mighty power. Put on all of God's armor so that you will be able to stand firm against all strategies of the devil [to undermine your

> commitment to your husband and divide the two of you]. For we are not fighting against flesh-and-blood enemies, but against evil rulers and authorities of the unseen world, against mighty powers in this dark world, and against evil spirits in the heavenly places [apparent in those situations in which you say something, he hears something else, and you wonder, *Is there someone in this room we can't see who is distorting everything that's being said?*].
>
> Therefore, put on every piece of God's armor so you will be able to resist the enemy [and the suggestions he makes to your thought life] in the time of evil. Then after the battle you will still be standing firm. Stand your ground, putting on the belt of truth and the body armor of God's righteousness. For shoes, put on the peace that comes from the Good News so that you will be fully prepared. In addition to all of these, hold up the shield of faith to stop the fiery arrows of the devil [when he launches an assault physically or mentally]. Put on salvation as your helmet [to guard the assault on your mind] and take the sword of the Spirit, which is the word of God.
>
> Pray in the Spirit at all times and on every occasion. Stay alert and be persistent in your prayers for all believers everywhere [including your husband and other couples as well] (Ephesians 6:10-18 NLT).

In our book *When Couples Walk Together*, Hugh and I addressed the spiritual battle couples face and encouraged our readers that "putting on the armor of God is nothing less than adorning yourself in the character of Jesus Christ. Each piece of the armor makes reference to an aspect of Christ's nature or character…So as you go through the process of 'suiting up,' keep in mind that as a couple you are not fighting your battles alone. You can recruit the supernatural power of the Son of God as you face the lion who wants to devour you" (1 Peter 5:8).[1] You can also ward off that attack that seeks to divide you by emanating the character of Christ toward your spouse.

Putting on the armor of God is nothing less than adorning yourself in the character of Jesus Christ.

Canceling the Contingencies

Relationships can get to the point where one or the other keeps a contingency in the back of their minds, thinking, *If he ever does that again, I'm outta here.* Whether it starts out as an annoying habit that turns into a large hurdle after time or it's something significant that rocks the relationship, living with an "if" keeps one foot out the door. Are you holding on to something that your husband could do that would make you walk away? Eliminate from your heart and mind the contingencies you believe would be deal-breakers. God holds no such reservations about you. Once you become His adopted child (through faith in Christ alone), there is nothing you can do for God to un-parent you. He sticks with you and continues to equip you to be the child He designed you to be.

Living with an "if" keeps one foot out the door.

God loves us with 1 Corinthians 13:7-8 love: "[He] bears all things, believes all things, hopes all things, endures all things. [God's] love never fails" (NASB). Let your husband know that no matter what, you will stick it out with him.

Applying the Glue

Hugh and I coined a phrase several years ago when we wrote *When Couples Walk Together*: "Grace is the glue that holds the two of you together." That phrase has helped us—and thousands of couples—find the adhesive that will make our "promise of forever" stick.

"Grace is the glue that holds the two of you together."

Life sends deterrents. If it hasn't already, it will. But you have Someone you can depend on who is greater than your circumstances and who wants your marriage not only to work but be wonderful. In fact, God wants your marriage to succeed even more than you do. He is fighting for you. And when you call upon Him for help, He will move heaven and earth to come through for you. Circumstances in life can definitely interrupt your honeymoon, but they can't take away your happily ever after if you are determined to stick it out. If you want to experience more with your husband, remember these three things:

- God wants to bless your marriage today just as much as you sensed His blessing on the day the two of you married.
- God is greater than any circumstance that might try to interfere, damage, or destroy your marriage.
- God can redeem, restore, and renew your heart to think and act like a new bride, just as much as He can redeem, restore, and renew the heart of your husband to respond to you the way He once did.

Grace—God's grace toward you and your grace toward each other—is the glue that holds the two of you together.

PRAYING IT THROUGH

Lord, I long to be a woman of my word and a woman of YOUR Word and keep my commitment to my husband. While that is so easy when I look at him through the eyes of love, there are times life gets difficult and I look at him through the eyes of accusation, disappointment, and past wounds. Lord, help me see my husband as You see him. Help me see him as I want him to see me. And help me see our union as one that You will fight for as we surrender it to You.

YOUR FOCUS FOR THE WEEK

Choose one of the strategies on pages 161-163 and focus on it this week. You may want to discuss it with your husband so the two of you can be battle-ready when the assaults come your way. Agree with him on a way that the two of you can continue to honor and respect one another, even when you disagree.

12

Bring It Back

Returning to the Way Things Used to Be

You are altogether beautiful, my darling;
there is no flaw in you.

Song of Songs 4:7

Think back to the day you fell in love with your husband. What was it about him that stole your heart?

Was it his smile, his sense of humor, the way he could make you laugh? Was it his gentleness toward you that made you feel cherished and loved? Was it his integrity and his determination to love you as God does?

Earlier this year I led a seminar called "Drawing Your Husband's Heart Closer to Yours." It was attended by wives of all ages who had been married anywhere from a few months to more than 40 years. The one common goal in the room was that each of those wives wanted to get their marriage back to the way it was when they started. As one 35-year-old wife told me, "All I want is for my husband to see me the way he did when we first married."

But for our husbands to see us as at our best, we need to be able to see them at their best. And often that starts when we initiate the process of bringing back the love and the feelings that were once there.

It's been said that whatever first attracted you to your spouse is often the thing that irritates you about him later. But when we trace back what is irritating us to why we fell in love with him in the first place, it reminds us of whom we married and why, and will help us bring back that loving feeling.

I am convinced, though, that in order to return to the way things used to be in our marriages, we ultimately need God—the only One who can redeem, restore, and renew love in our hearts.

When Love Fades

God knows what it's like to be on the receiving end of a once-passionate love that has faded through the years. Listen to His heartfelt words spoken centuries ago to His beloved bride, the church:

God knows what it's like to be on the receiving end of a once-passionate love that has faded through the years.

> I know your deeds, your hard work and your perseverance. I know that you cannot tolerate wicked people, that you have tested those who claim to be apostles but are not, and have found them false. You have persevered and have endured hardships for my name, and have not grown weary (Revelation 2:2-3).

So far, so good, right? He is commending her for her hard work and her loyalty. But her "acts of service" aren't enough. God can't be fooled. He's sees something missing, and He wants it back:

> Yet I hold this against you: You have forsaken the love you had at first. Consider how far you have fallen! Repent and do the things you did at first (Revelation 2:4-5).

Can you hear the plea in God's voice: *You don't love Me the way you used to. Remember how you were so high on My love? You were on the heights! Now look at where you are...you've sunken into the valley of complacency. Do the things you used to do and love Me the way you once did.*

In the Contemporary English Version, that passage reads like this:

> I know everything you have done, including your hard work and how you have endured...You have endured and gone through hard times because of me, and you have not given up.
>
> But I do have something against you! And it is this: You don't have as much love as you used to. Think about where you have fallen from, and then turn back and do as you did at first (Revelation 2:2-5).

The Root of the Problem

God diagnosed the heart of His lover (the church): She was going through the motions, but her heart wasn't really into it. He instructed her in how to get her heart back for Him. He told her to

- Remember how high her feelings were for Him.
- Realize how far she had fallen.
- Repent for losing that loving feeling.
- Return to the things she used to do.

Do you remember the way you and your husband once were? Do you realize how far *you* might have fallen from what you used to do? Can you repent for letting other loves steal your heart away (your love for your job; your love for your children; your love of "being in love"; your love for how he used to make you feel; your love for food, shopping, working out, or whatever it is that you might now crave more than him)? And can you return to the things you used to do for him?

There is much we can apply to our own marriages today from this letter of God's to His church. But first let's look at my cousin Lisa's story of a marriage that God wouldn't let die.

Waiting for It to End

Lisa was a 27-year-old single mom of one young son when she

married Jason, a father of five children aged 8 to 16. A year later they had a baby together, but there wasn't much of a sense of togetherness.

"If it weren't for my faith and beliefs, I would have more than happily divorced the moment I began to be unhappy," Lisa said. "My marriage wouldn't have made it to year two before I would have called it quits."

But seeking to honor God, out of an attempt to keep her conscience clear, ended up saving her marriage.

I'll let Lisa tell you her story in her own words:

"When Jason and I married we thought we knew each other pretty well. But by the second year of our marriage, neither of us wanted to be married to the other anymore. We were each waiting for the other to leave and didn't realize the other person felt that way. We had narrow blinders on that gave us the impression that we were being wronged and didn't deserve the unhappiness that we both felt.

"With all the stress and expectations and drama that goes with blended families (and I think our drama was on the higher end), our attitudes toward each other became very comfortable in a bad way. We wouldn't hold back our disdain when one of us failed to meet the other's expectations. We each blamed the other for changing.

"I remember at that time reading a book that mentioned that men saw working long hours and putting in overtime as a way to provide for their family and show their love. Many of the wives interviewed took it as 'he would rather be at work than spend time with me.' The author suggested letting your husband know how much you appreciate the work he does for your family. I figured my marriage had already failed by that point, and I didn't feel the desire to do it, but I sent my husband a text message anyway thanking him for all his hard work and for providing for the family. His response? 'What did I do wrong now?'

"I felt *terrible*. Was appreciation from me such a foreign concept to him that he didn't know how to take it? I resolved to continue to show that I appreciated him. He was very wary at first.

"I believe our biggest breakthrough in our marriage came when I stopped telling my husband what *we* needed to work on and started focusing on what I needed to do myself. I stopped pushing him toward quiet times with God, toward hanging out with godly men, toward getting involved in men's groups. I stopped pushing him to become the husband I wanted. Instead, I focused on me and my relationship with God. I figured if Jason left me, my conscience would be clear and my relationship with God would be bullet-proof. However, Jason noticed that I wasn't trying to change him any longer and he stopped fighting back. He began to slowly but actively search for those things himself. He began to read his Bible more and started to become the spiritual leader of our family I had hoped he would strive to be. He began to set aside a date night for just the two of us every week. He started again trying to sweep me off of my feet. He told me that it was because he had seen the change in me.

"Jason and I started attending a couple's group at church Sunday mornings that gave us homework, asking us some hard questions about things you normally keep to yourself (or discuss with your girlfriends or he discusses with his buddies). The difficult part was sharing those answers with my husband. He also shared answers I didn't want to hear. The important part was that the walls came down.

"As we grew in our commitment toward each other, we eventually became leaders of a small group for couples, and we have continued to learn how to better communicate with one another and to show each other respect.

"Our passion seems to increase with each trial and heartache we've come up against. I remember when our oldest child told us she was pregnant and wanted to marry her boyfriend. My heart sank as I realized that might be the final nail in the coffin of our marriage. To my surprise, my husband reached over and held my hand, telling me it was going to be okay. He assured me we would be able to get through all of this together.

"We have learned to come together to support each other emotionally, which has increased our trust and understanding of each other."

In many ways Lisa wouldn't want to return to the way it used to be when she and Jason were newlyweds. She realizes that all she and her husband have gone through has made them stronger.

"We've found strength in our faith in God and in relying on each other," Lisa said. "It has given us a newfound love and respect for each other. Even when I remember his sweeping romantic gestures during our courtship, I can honestly say that I much prefer this man and how he treats me and looks at me *now* than when we first married. We never had an effortless part of our marriage, but I can say that it has been well worth all the ups and downs since we have learned to ride those waves together."

From Broken to Better

Sometimes when we don't see an improvement, we assume our marriage will never get better. But couples like Lisa and Jason will tell you "it sometimes has to get worse before it gets better." Don't be afraid to reach your breaking point. It is often when we are broken, out of options, and fully dependent on God that we finally surrender to His design for our marriage. And then He takes our broken pieces and, through His grace, glues us back together into the humble, God-honoring couple that He desires. Remember, grace is the glue that holds the two of you together—God's grace for both of you, and your grace toward each other.

Don't be afraid to reach your breaking point. It is often when we are broken, out of options, and fully dependent on God that we finally surrender to His design for our marriage.

Recharge the Romance

The longer you and your husband remain together, the longer you collect a history—a history rich with experience, lessons learned, and opportunities to show each other grace. You've been learning how to do life together, and that is precious. And just remembering all you've been through together can help usher you both to a place of renewed intimacy. I asked several healthy, grace-glued couples to share with you what they have done or focused on through the years to keep the fires of passion burning for one another and to keep their commitment to each other. As you read through this list of advice you may find it helpful to draw a smiley face next to the suggestions you are doing now, and a heart or check mark next to the ones you want to try or still need to work on.

The longer you and your husband remain together, the longer you collect a history—a history rich with experience, lessons learned, and opportunities to show each other grace.

Rediscover Your "Us"

Robin, the marriage and family counselor I referred to in chapters 4 and 8, and her husband, Jeff, who is also a marriage and family counselor, are rediscovering each other and how much they enjoy being together now that their youngest child has left home and it's just the two of them again.

"In the last five years as we enter into the new season of our marriage as empty nesters, we have discovered our new 'us.'

"After persevering through some difficult seasons, we are stronger than we've ever been, we are more connected, and we have a deeper understanding and appreciation of one another.

"Our 'us' is neither completely like me nor my husband, but it is this third species that seeks the best for the purpose of the marriage. It is a new creation, much like a child, that has its own unique purpose and shared interest for the sake of pleasing the Lord. For example, I love to attend musicals and the theatre, but my husband loves to attend professional baseball games. But our new 'us' loves to go hiking and mountain biking. We value 'us' more than we value our individual likes or hobbies. We seek the growth of the marriage over our individual interests. I now love to go to baseball games because I am able to share the joy of my husband's childhood pastime and enjoy him and our special time together."

Reinvest in Each Other

You don't have to wait until your kids are out of the house, though, to invest in your "us." You can start reinvesting in each other right now.

Connie said this is how she is able to experience more with her husband, Tyler:

"It isn't that we have *one thing* that has brought us closer together, but there is something that we've done continually that builds trust, passion, and communication between us. At least once a year we do something marriage-focused: attend a conference, be a part of a small group, or lead a marriage group. When we come together on a given night of the week or weekend to serve or sit next to each other in a group listening to a video or teachers, we grow closer together. As we grow closer, our trust, passion, and communication increases.

"During these times, we go through homework and group questions. We listen. We open up. We pray together. We enjoy each other. We hug and hold hands. We are drawn together by drawing closer to the Lord, side by side.

"I'm usually eager to book the next small group opportunity before the current one ends because it feels so good to be in that place."

Refocus on Intimacy

Allison said getaways (even on a budget) have been so important in her 33-year marriage to Guy. "They recharge your romance, and can give clarity and perspective about how your focus or direction may have changed," she said. "Get away and refocus yourself on your intimacy and making great love memories to tide you over during dry or hard days to come. Be extravagant in showing your love to each other, even though the cost does not have to be extravagant. It pays huge returns in the short term *and* the long term."

Get away and refocus yourself on making great love memories to tide you over during dry or hard days to come.

In an article by J. Parker called "4 Reasons You Need to Go on a Second Honeymoon,"[1] she cites that getting away with your spouse decreases your stress, deepens your friendship, increases your sexual intimacy, and reminds you why you got married.

"When you get away for that second honeymoon, guess what you get to do? Act like newlyweds!" Parker wrote. "Or, to tell the truth, you're likely better lovers now than you were back when. Many couples report increased sexual satisfaction a decade or more into their marriage. In the time since you said I do, you've learned a lot about your body, his body, and how your bodies fit together. And if you haven't, a second honeymoon is a great time for discovery or rediscovery…. In the usual busyness of life, we can forget what attracted us to one another. We get used to each other and perhaps take our relationship for granted. But taking a second honeymoon can remind you exactly why you committed your love and life to your spouse."

Recommit to One Another

Barbara said she and Don reread their wedding vows to one another on every wedding anniversary—"sometimes in the restaurant over dinner (yes, we take them with us), or at home if we don't go out." This was her husband's idea, and they have been doing it since their first anniversary. If you don't have written-down vows, then write new ones and share them with each other. For a man, there's nothing quite like hearing his wife would still say "I do" to him all over again.

Reach Out and Touch

Reaching out for his hand says to him, "I want to be near you" and "I want others to know I am with you."

My brother, Steve, says his wife helps bring him back to their early years "when she takes the initiative to hold hands or be close to me when we are out."

A friend of mine, who has been married more than 30 years, makes a constant effort to build up her husband through both affirming words and gentle touch.

"Because I believe my husband's love language is both words of encouragement and physical touch, it is important that I grab his hand and tell him I enjoy being with him," she said. "Sometimes I feel resentful because I want *him* to make that effort. So I continue to work on that through very creative ways. For instance, I am exhausted when I get home from work, and I've usually talked so much on my job that I have used up all my words. Yet my husband is Italian Portuguese and never runs out of words! So even if I just sit with him and nod he is good. It's difficult to give my all at work all day and come home and act interested. So most of the time I say something like, 'Give me 15 minutes to wash my face and get comfy and then I am all yours!'"

Revisit Fun

It's a tragedy when life becomes so busy that you and your husband don't have time to have fun anymore.

After being married to Bob for almost 45 years, Dawn Marie now realizes how important it is for the two of them to laugh often and have fun together.

"For so many years, I allowed the busyness of life to make me far too serious. In recent years I've tried to recapture those early days of companionship when we enjoyed each other's company, laughed together, and simply smiled at each other.

"Recently, when he was watching television, I sat on the couch opposite him, grinning. Finally, he asked, 'What?' I shared that he was talking in his sleep the night before and how that reminded me of a funny story from early in our marriage. He knew exactly what I meant and grinned. On a ministry team, Bob was in a skit for teenagers that called for another team member to smack him in the face with a huge powdery powder puff. Later that night, as we fell into exhausted sleep, my hubby suddenly sat up in bed and yelled, *'Makeup!'* It scared me to death! We still laugh out loud when we remember that night. I think remembering those early days of marriage—especially the fun and sweet times—can help our spouse respond to the newlywed spirit that may be buried deep inside."

Think about what used to make the two of you laugh and recreate it. Revisit memories that drew the two of you together. Reinvent some new, exciting habits like five-minute back and neck massages during your spouse's favorite television program. Each of you wants to feel desired by the other, so write something romantic on a sticky note and place it where only your spouse will see it and blush. Start a weekly date night incorporating something each time that was once meaningful to one or both of you. Be creative and make it happen.

Think about what used to make the two of you laugh and recreate it.

Reminisce About Yesteryear

Allison suggested, "Take time regularly (or at least once a year on an anniversary retreat get-away) to reminisce about how you met, dated, fell in love, and what you have loved about each other over the years. Take time to have specific conversations about how things may have changed and how you would like to see things change to make your marriage better. Go there with even the hard conversations when you have time to share your thoughts." Allison's suggestion is another way to connect and bring things back to the days when you were constantly monitoring your relationship.

Remember to Flirt

I'm certain every one of us loved it when our husbands flirted with us back in the day. So bring that back by continuing to flirt with him today. Debbie said, "I intentionally continue to flirt with my husband! I have determined to remain playful, and I look for ways to have fun with him and with our family. But perhaps most importantly, I intentionally speak words of encouragement, affirmation, and respect every day (which can come in the form of flirting or gentle encouragement). This alone draws my husband's heart closer to mine. I mean, who wouldn't want to be around a person who is constantly encouraging you and pointing out your good qualities?"

Recognize and Celebrate Your Differences

Greg and Julie Gorman, coauthors of *Two Are Better Than One: God Has a Purpose for Your Marriage*, wrote in their book, "One of the greatest opportunities presented in marriage is appreciating our spouse's differences—not just tolerating them, but actually celebrating them."[2]

Julie reiterated this when she told me the key to her and Greg's connection: "We learned the value of celebrating our differences rather than exhausting our efforts trying to change one another," she said. "It's all about perspective. When I feel like I'm getting the short end of the stick, I remember to look at Greg as a gift that I get to unwrap every day. I spend my life trying to *discover* him like I did when we first dated. I talk about things that I know will interest him. As I spend my life trying to understand what he loves, he reciprocates. *Always* look at him through the eyes of when you first dated."

Return to the "New Bride" Mentality

Remember the new bride in the Song of Songs that we looked at earlier in this book? I found it inspiring the way she talked to others about her husband, even after there was a rift between them. In Song 5:10-16 she sang:

> He is handsome and healthy,
> the most outstanding
>   among ten thousand.
> His head is purest gold;
> his hair is wavy,
>   black as a raven.
> His eyes are a pair of doves
> bathing in a stream
>   flowing with milk.[a]
> His face is a garden
>   of sweet-smelling spices;

his lips are lilies
    dripping with perfume.

His arms are branches of gold
    covered with jewels;
his body is ivory[b]
    decorated with sapphires.
His legs are columns of marble
    on feet of gold.
He stands there majestic
like Mount Lebanon
    and its choice cedar trees.
His kisses are sweet.
    I desire him so much!
Young women of Jerusalem,
    he is my lover and friend (CEV).

Again, this passage comes shortly after a misunderstanding between them, and she was convicted that she had grown complacent and was not responding to him as she once had. She immediately launched into what she loved about him after being at odds with him. I believe that is a good lesson for us. When we start responding to our husbands like we would respond to just about anyone (or worse than we'd respond to anyone), we need to remember what it is we love about him, what first attracted us to him, and focus on that, not on whatever is causing the upset.

Ladies, that is the easiest and quickest way to regain that spark for our husbands: to remember the reason we fell in love, to remember what first drew our hearts to him, and to focus on that, not on what drove us temporarily apart.

Did you also notice how she ended that description?

He is altogether lovely [there's the generous
    summarization of it all]
This is my beloved, this is my friend (Song of Songs 5:16).

She realized not only was he her lover (as passionate romantic love can tend to fade over time) but he was her *friend*—the one who knew her better than anyone, the one she had given herself to completely, the one whom she *loved*.

The day you married your husband you truly believed he was altogether lovely. He is the same man, even though you might focus now on things you'd rather he *not* do. If our husbands are not altogether lovely anymore, then maybe you and I are the ones who have changed—changed our focus, changed our perspective, changed what we choose to see.

I mentioned in chapter 4 that love is blind—blind to her lover's failures, weaknesses, and warts. Be blind to your husband's less attractive traits. Choose to see what is best in him. And chances are he will begin to see what is best in you as well.

Love—God's Way

I believe the best way we can bring back that loving feeling between us and our husbands is to love them God's way. Not our way, which is often conditional, one-sided, dependent upon our moods and our own happiness. But *God's* way—unconditionally and sacrificially.

Arguably the best description of love is found in the Bible in 1 Corinthians 13. It is a passage that is often quoted at weddings, even by those who aren't believers. Because God is the author of love, I truly believe this description of love is the description of Him. So I want to put God's name in place of the word *love* (and every reference to the word *love*) throughout this passage so you can not only understand more fully how God loves *you*, but how He loves your husband as well and, more importantly, how He expects *you* to love your husband:

> God is patient, God is kind. God does not envy, God does not boast, God is not proud. God does not dishonor others, God is not self-seeking, God is not easily angered, God keeps no record of wrongs. God does not delight in evil but rejoices with the truth. God always protects, always trusts, always hopes, always perseveres.
>
> God never fails.

What can you and I learn from this? God is patient with our husbands' shortcomings and enduring in His love for our husbands, and we must be too. I know I need to practice patience and kindness toward Hugh and not keep a record of his wrongs. I need to always protect, always trust, always hope in him, and always persevere in my love for him.

I especially like the way verse 7 reads in the New American Standard Bible: "[Love] bears all things, believes all things, hopes all things, endures all things."

Can you be a wife who *bears all things* when it comes to your husband's shortcomings, *believes all things* good about your husband even when he's slipped up, *hopes all things* simply because he hasn't given up on you, and *endures all things* with him? Christ endured all things for you—even death on a cross—so you could live with Him eternally. Love your husband *God's* way and you will have the kind of love that endures through the years.

The Words I'd Been Waiting For

Somehow this book would feel incomplete if I didn't end it by telling you this: *It happened.* The words I'd been wanting to read, the words I'd been *waiting* to read—the words I wondered if I'd *ever* read again—stared at me in the handwriting I've come to love through the years.

Hugh started his letter with, *To my forever and only love* and, instead of talking about who I *used* to be, he wrote—in words so close to my heart that I can't write them here—how precious our togetherness is in spite of the ups, downs, challenges, and wear and tear through the years. He ended his letter with:

> *I love our story, and I love you, always have, always will.*
>
> *Your husband,*
> *—Hugh*

Tears filled my eyes as I realized I was reading the evidence that I had truly become the woman he had fallen in love with three decades ago. Or maybe he finally realized he loved just as much—or even more—this older, thicker, hopefully wiser, and definitely more wrinkled woman that I am today.

Honestly, if I could make my husband see me the way he once did, you can too. By applying what you've read here, chapter by chapter, and revisiting those areas where you still feel you need work, you can convince him that you are still the best thing on this earth that's ever happened to him.

SEEING IT THROUGH

Now it's your turn. As I alluded to at the beginning of this chapter, the easiest way to fall back in love with your man is to remember what first drew you to him. Deep down, underneath all that has transpired between the two of you, he is still the same man. He just needs you to be the same woman so he can remember what he felt about you. I challenge you to be that woman who caught his eye, who had eyes just for him, and who was not content until he was yours.

Be that woman again—with God's help—and experience more with your husband. More trust. More passion. More communication. And more than you thought was possible.

YOUR FOCUS FOR THE WEEK

After your husband has had a nice dinner, share with him the list of suggestions to "Recharge the Romance" on pages 175-183. Show him the ones you put smiley faces next to (that you two seem to be doing well) and the ones you put a heart or a check mark next to (that you both need to work on). Ask for his input on what he feels you two are doing well and what he thinks should be worked on too. Then take the lead to pray this prayer with him:

> *Lord, thank You for the gift of each other and the privilege we have to share life together. Thank You for the ways You have helped us connect as a couple thus far. Thank You, too, that it*

is so important to You that we have a strong marriage that You have provided tools and resources and ideas from other couples to help us along on our journey. God, help us to ___________

____

______________________________(fill in one or two of the suggestions that you need work on) *so we can grow closer together and ultimately glorify You. Thank You that You are going before us on this journey and You are guiding us every step of the way. In Christ's name, amen.*

Additional Resources to Help You Experience More

Self-Assessment: How Far Have You Come?

Now that we've spent 12 chapters together and you've been learning ways to die to self, put him first, and ultimately experience more with your husband, let's see how far you've come. Take this test you took in the introduction of this book and then compare your results. Once again, circle "yes" for the answers that most often describe you and "no" for the ones that most often don't.

I expect my husband to meet most, if not all, of my emotional needs.	Yes / No
When I do something for my husband, I expect the same in return.	Yes / No
I tend to be focused more on my needs than my husband's.	Yes / No
I was a lot more attentive to my husband when we were first married.	Yes / No

If I'm not careful I can put the needs of my job/children/parents before my husband.	Yes / No
I paid a lot more attention to how I looked, dressed, and behaved before I was married.	Yes / No
I tend to hover when my husband is watching the kids or working on something for me.	Yes / No
I can tend to slip into "mother mode" with my husband without realizing it.	Yes / No
I can't stand to be away from my husband. I want him close by all the time.	Yes / No
I tend to do things the same every time. Spontaneity is not my strength.	Yes / No
I have a hard time letting some things go, especially if they hurt me deeply.	Yes / No
I sometimes wish my husband was more like (fill in the blank here).	Yes / No
I fantasize, at times, about an ex-boyfriend/fiancé/husband.	Yes / No
I resent not being able to understand *why* my husband acts a certain way.	Yes / No
I am quick to point out when my husband offends me.	Yes / No
I want to "talk it out" every time something is bothering me.	Yes / No
I insist on a resolution when we talk about our issues.	Yes / No

I prefer to be silent when something is bothering me.	Yes / No
I avoid conflict by withdrawing emotionally or leaving the room.	Yes / No
I have been known to "storm out" when there is conflict.	Yes / No
I expect to be my husband's top priority, as he is mine.	Yes / No
I've said or thought the words "I've had it!" when it comes to my husband.	Yes / No
I have one or more contingencies under which I would leave the relationship.	Yes / No
I rarely consult my husband about my personal plans or dreams.	Yes / No
Because of pain in my past I am easily triggered by things my husband says to me.	Yes / No

How did you do? Did some of your "yes" answers change to "no" now that you've been reading about how to experience more with your husband? If there are still areas where you need work, surrender those areas to God and ask for His help in dying to self, putting your husband's needs above your own, and trusting that God will honor you as you choose to honor Him and your spouse.

Dying to Self in Your Marriage

Dying to self and surrendering your marriage to God first involves surrendering to God personally, and in every way. God, being holy and without sin, demands that we surrender our lives to Him by repenting of our sin and accepting His Son as our means to forgiveness and righteousness. We are people with a sin problem (Romans 3:23), and it manifests itself in our pride that wants to live our lives how we want rather than how our Maker wants. Before we can give our marriage to God and have Him meet us there, we must give to Him our sin problem so He can put us in the position where He can help us.

To surrender to God, you must

1. Admit you are a sinner by nature and there is nothing you can do on your own to make up for that sin in the eyes of a holy God.
2. Accept the sacrifice that God provided—the death of His sinless Son, Jesus, on the cross on your behalf—in order to bring yourself into communion with Him.
3. Enter into a love relationship with God, through Jesus, as a response to His love and forgiveness toward you.[1]
4. Surrender to God your right to yourself and acknowledge

His right to carry out His plans for you and to mold you, shape you, and transform you for His pleasure.

5. Find a pastor or women's ministry director at a Bible-believing church in your area or a trusted Christian friend and tell him or her of your decision to surrender your life to Christ. They will want to pray for you and get you the support you need to grow in your new relationship with Christ.
6. Now surrender your marriage to God by acknowledging that He is in control of every area of your life and that He can bring your marriage into alignment with His will. Ask for the grace to die to self so that your husband can see Christ in you and is convicted to surrender his life to Christ as well, if he hasn't already.

If you went through these six steps and are now in a saving relationship with Christ, I'd love to hear about it. Contact me at Cindi@StrengthForTheSoul.com or through a letter sent to the address listed on page 219 called "An Invitation to Write."

Scriptural Encouragement for Difficult Days

Reason for Our Pain or Struggles

We know that all things work together for good to those who love God, to those who are the called according to His purpose. For whom he foreknew, He also predestined to become conformed to the image of His Son (Romans 8:28-29 NKJV).

Blessed be the God and Father of our Lord Jesus Christ, the Father of mercies and God of all comfort, who comforts us in all our tribulation, that we may be able to comfort those who are in any trouble, with the comfort with which we ourselves are comforted by God (2 Corinthians 1:3-4 NKJV).

My brethren, count it all joy when you fall into various trials, knowing that the testing of your faith produces patience. But let patience have its perfect work, that you may be perfect and complete, lacking nothing (James 1:2-4 NKJV).

God's Purpose and Sovereignty

As for you, you meant evil against me; but God meant it for good (Genesis 50:20 NKJV).

"For My thoughts are not your thoughts,
Nor are your ways My ways," says the LORD.
"For as the heavens are higher than the earth,
So are My ways higher than your ways,
And My thoughts than your thoughts (Isaiah 55:8-9 NKJV).

The LORD gave another message to Jeremiah. He said, "Go down to the potter's shop, and I will speak to you while there." So I did as he told me and found the potter working at his wheel. But the jar he was making did not turn out as he had hoped, so he crushed it into a lump of clay and started over.

Then the LORD gave me this message: "O Israel, can I not do to you as this potter has done to his clay? As the clay is in the potter's hand, so are you in my hand" (Jeremiah 18:1-6 NLT).

For our light affliction, which is but for a moment, is working for us a far more exceeding and eternal weight of glory, while we do not look at the things which are seen, but at the things which are not seen. For the things which are seen are temporary, but the things which are not seen are eternal (2 Corinthians 4:17-18 NKJV).

Cleansing and Forgiveness

I acknowledged my sin to You,
And my iniquity I have not hidden.
I said, "I will confess my transgressions to the LORD,"
And You forgave the iniquity of my sin (Psalm 32:5 NKJV).

Have mercy upon me, O God,
According to Your lovingkindness;
According to the multitude of Your tender mercies,
Blot out my transgressions.
Wash me thoroughly from my iniquity,
And cleanse me from my sin (Psalm 51:1-2 NKJV).

As far as the east is from the west,
So far has He removed our transgressions from us (Psalm 103:12 NKJV).

Search me, O God, and know my heart;
Try me, and know my anxieties;
And see if there is any wicked way in me,
And lead me in the way everlasting (Psalm 139:23-24 NKJV).

I, even I, am He who blots out your transgressions for My own sake; and I will not remember your sins (Isaiah 43:25 NKJV).

I will forgive their iniquity, and their sin I will remember no more (Jeremiah 31:34 NKJV).

You will again have compassion on us;
you will tread our sins underfoot
and hurl all our iniquities into the depths of the sea (Micah 7:19).

Therefore, as the elect of God, holy and beloved, put on tender mercies, kindness, humility, meekness, longsuffering; bearing with one another, and forgiving one another, if anyone has a complaint against another; even as Christ forgave you, so you also must do (Colossians 3:12-13 NKJV).

If we confess our sins, He is faithful and just to forgive us our sins and to cleanse us from all unrighteousness (1 John 1:9 NKJV).

Comfort and Deliverance

I will both lie down in peace, and sleep;
For You alone, O LORD, make me dwell in safety (Psalm 4:8 NKJV).

His anger is but for a moment,
His favor is for life;
Weeping may endure for a night,
But joy comes in the morning (Psalm 30:5 NKJV).

You are my hiding place;
You shall preserve me from trouble;
You shall surround me with songs of deliverance (Psalm 32:7 NKJV).

I waited patiently for the LORD;

And He inclined to me,
And heard my cry.
He also brought me up out of a horrible pit,
Out of the miry clay,
And set my feet upon a rock,
And established my steps.
He has put a new song in my mouth—
Praise to our God;
Many will see it and fear,
And will trust in the LORD (Psalm 40:1-3 NKJV).

God is our refuge and strength,
A very present help in trouble.
Therefore we will not fear,
Even though the earth be removed,
And though the mountains be carried into the midst of the sea;
Though its waters roar and be troubled,
Though the mountains shake with its swelling (Psalm 46:1-3 NKJV).

Trust in Him at all times, you people;
Pour out your heart before Him;
God is a refuge for us (Psalm 62:8 NKJV).

My help comes from the LORD,
Who made heaven and earth.
He will not allow your foot to be moved;
He who keeps you will not slumber (Psalm 121:2-3 NKJV).

Where can I go from Your Spirit?
Or where can I flee from Your presence?
If I ascend into heaven, You are there;
If I make my bed in hell, behold, You are there.
If I take the wings of the morning,
And dwell in the uttermost parts of the sea,
Even there Your hand shall lead me,
And Your right hand shall hold me.
If I say, "Surely the darkness shall fall on me,"
Even the night shall be light about me;

Indeed, the darkness shall not hide from You,
But the night shines as the day;
The darkness and the light are both alike to You (Psalm 139:7-12 NKJV).

The LORD is gracious and full of compassion,
Slow to anger and great in mercy.
The LORD is good to all,
And His tender mercies are over all His works (Psalm 145:8-9 NKJV).

When you pass through the waters, I will be with you;
And through the rivers, they shall not overflow you.
When you walk through the fire, you shall not be burned,
Nor shall the flame scorch you (Isaiah 43:2).

For I know the thoughts that I think toward you, says the LORD, thoughts of peace and not of evil, to give you a future and a hope (Jeremiah 29:11 NKJV).

The LORD has appeared of old to me, saying:
"Yes, I have loved you with an everlasting love;
Therefore with lovingkindness I have drawn you" (Jeremiah 31:3 NKJV).

I am convinced that nothing can ever separate us from God's love. Neither death nor life, neither angels nor demons, neither our fears for today nor our worries about tomorrow—not even the powers of hell can separate us from God's love. No power in the sky above or in the earth below—indeed, nothing in all creation will ever be able to separate us from the love of God that is revealed in Christ Jesus our Lord (Romans 8:38-39 NLT).

Blessed be the God and Father of our Lord Jesus Christ, the Father of mercies and God of all comfort, who comforts us in all our tribulation, that we may be able to comfort those who are in any trouble, with the comfort with which we ourselves are comforted by God (2 Corinthians 1:3-4 NKJV).

He Himself has said, "I will never leave you nor forsake you" (Hebrews 13:5 NKJV).

Comfort in the Face of Death

Even though I walk through the valley of the shadow of death,
I will fear no evil,
for you are with me;
your rod and your staff,
they comfort me (Psalm 23:4 ESV).

Precious in the sight of the LORD
Is the death of His saints (Psalm 116:15 NKJV).

The LORD cares deeply
when his loved ones die (Psalm 116:15 NLT).

Jesus said to her, "I am the resurrection and the life. He who believes in Me, though he may die, he shall live. And whoever lives and believes in Me shall never die" (John 11:25-26 NKJV).

And if I go and prepare a place for you, I will come again and receive you to Myself; that where I am, there you may be also (John 14:3 NKJV).

God's Provision

The young lions lack and suffer hunger;
But those who seek the LORD shall not lack any good thing (Psalm 34:10 NKJV).

The LORD God is a sun and shield;
The LORD will give grace and glory;
No good thing will He withhold
From those who walk uprightly (Psalm 84:11 NKJV).

The LORD upholds all who fall,
And raises up all who are bowed down.
The eyes of all look expectantly to You,
And You give them their food in due season.
You open Your hand
And satisfy the desire of every living thing (Psalm 145:14-16 NKJV).

And my God shall supply all your need according to His riches in glory by Christ Jesus (Philippians 4:19 NKJV).

Healing

He heals the brokenhearted
And binds up their wounds (Psalm 147:3 NKJV).

Surely he has borne our griefs
And carried our sorrows;
Yet we esteemed Him stricken,
Smitten by God, and afflicted.
But He was wounded for our transgressions,
He was bruised for our iniquities;
The chastisement for our peace was upon Him,
And by His stripes we are healed (Isaiah 53:4-5 NKJV).

The Spirit of the LORD is upon Me,
Because He has anointed Me
To preach the gospel to the poor;
He has sent Me to heal the brokenhearted,
To proclaim liberty to the captives
And recovery of sight to the blind
To set at liberty those who are oppressed (Luke 4:18 NKJV).

Restoration

Create in me a clean heart, O God,
And renew a steadfast spirit within me.
Do not cast me away from Your presence,
And do not take Your Holy Spirit from me.
Restore to me the joy of Your salvation,
And uphold me by Your generous Spirit (Psalm 51:10-12 NKJV).

I will give you a new heart and put a new spirit within you; I will take the heart of stone out of your flesh and give you a heart of flesh (Ezekiel 36:26 NKJV).

Anyone who belongs to Christ has become a new person. The old life is gone; a new life has begun! (2 Corinthians 5:17 NLT).

I have been crucified with Christ; it is no longer I who live, but Christ lives in me; and the life which I now live in the flesh I live by faith in the Son of God, who loved me and gave Himself for me (Galatians 2:20 NKJV).

Significance

You number my wanderings;
Put my tears into Your bottle;
Are they not in Your book? (Psalm 56:8 NKJV).

You formed my inward parts;
You covered me in my mother's womb.
I will praise You, for I am fearfully and wonderfully made;
Marvelous are Your works,
And that my soul knows very well.
My frame was not hidden from You,
When I was made in secret,
And skillfully wrought in the lowest parts of the earth.
Your eyes saw my substance, being yet unformed.
And in Your book they all were written,
The days fashioned for me,
When as yet there were none of them.

How precious also are Your thoughts to me, O God!
How great is the sum of them!
If I should count them, they would be more in number than the sand;
When I awake, I am still with You (Psalm 139:13-18 NKJV).

Can a woman forget her nursing child,
And not have compassion on the son of her womb?
Surely they may forget,
Yet I will not forget you.
See, I have inscribed you on the palms of My hands;
Your walls are continually before Me (Isaiah 49:15-16 NKJV).

Are not two sparrows sold for a copper coin? And not one of them falls to the ground apart from your Father's will. But the very hairs of your head are all numbered. Do not fear therefore; you are of more value than many sparrows (Matthew 10:29-31 NKJV).

Spiritual Strength

The weapons we fight with are not the weapons of the world. On the contrary, they have divine power to demolish strongholds. We demolish arguments and every pretension that sets itself up against the knowledge of God, and we take captive every thought to make it obedient to Christ (2 Corinthians 10:4-5).

Now to Him who is able to do exceedingly abundantly above all that we ask or think, according to the power that works in us (Ephesians 3:20 NKJV).

Finally, my brethren, be strong in the Lord and in the power of His might. Put on the whole armor of God, that you may be able to stand against the wiles of the devil. For we do not wrestle against flesh and blood, but against principalities, against powers, against the rulers of the darkness of this age, against spiritual hosts of wickedness in the heavenly places. Therefore take up the whole armor of God, that you may be able to withstand in the evil day, and having done all, to stand.

Stand therefore, having girded your waist with truth, having put on the breastplate of righteousness, and having shod your feet with the preparation of the gospel of peace; above all, taking the shield of faith with which you will be able to quench all the fiery darts of the wicked one. And take the helmet of salvation, and the sword of the Spirit, which is the word of God; praying always with all prayer and supplication in the Spirit, being watchful to this end with all perseverance and supplication for all the saints (Ephesians 6:10-18 NKJV).

Be anxious for nothing, but in everything by prayer and supplication, with thanksgiving, let your requests be made known to God; and the peace of God, which surpasses all understanding, will guard your hearts and minds through Christ Jesus (Philippians 4:6-7 NKJV).

Whatever is true, whatever is noble, whatever is right, whatever is pure, whatever is lovely whatever is admirable—if anything is excellent or praiseworthy—think about such things (Philippians 4:8).

I can do all things through Christ who strengthens me (Philippians 4:13 NKJV).

How to Encourage Your Husband to Pray with You

Admit it. You'd like to be one of those couples that prays together daily, conducts family devotions regularly, and models to others what a spiritual home should look like.

But if you're like us—and most couples we've talked to—you're not quite there. However, that doesn't mean you can't ever be.

Although my husband was a pastor for more than 20 years and I continue to be heavily involved in ministry too, it took us a good 20 years before we started setting aside time to pray together regularly. And when we did, we realized it was the single most important factor in creating a closer connection between the two of us.

And yet why did it take us so long to prioritize praying together? The reasons—or maybe I should say excuses—abounded.

As Hugh and I began researching and writing our book *When Couples Walk Together*, we interviewed many couples on the subject of praying together and learned we were not alone in our struggle. Nor were our reasons unique for finding it difficult to come together to pray.

The Schedule Dilemma

We found the number one reason most couples cited for not

praying together was conflicting schedules and the inability to find the time. For years, my husband and I cited this excuse too. He was up early and out the door for work while I was helping our daughter get ready for school, which made morning prayer together nearly impossible. And praying at night before bed was out of the question as he would fall asleep much earlier than I would. But we realized that we *make* the time to do what is most important to us, so we had to start getting creative in making time for prayer in our schedule. Other couples we talked to also struggled with making the time, but once they did, they found another difficulty arose.

The Intimidation Factor

In talking with many couples about why they don't pray together, the schedule is often the first excuse. But underneath that is the feeling that one's spirituality will be measured by the length or depth of one's prayers. Many wives expect their husbands, as the spiritual heads of the household, to initiate prayer, to comfort their hearts through prayer when they are feeling misunderstood, to be their spiritual strength. And those kinds of expectations can be intimidating to any man. Likewise, wives can feel intimidated too, if they feel their prayers don't match the spiritual depth of their husbands. Some spouses tend to be more verbose in their prayers, while others feel more comfortable internalizing their thoughts and praying silently to God. Prayer makes *anyone* feel vulnerable, especially if someone other than God is listening in.

The "Unseen" Battle

Finally, praying with one's spouse is difficult at times because the enemy of our souls doesn't want us praying together. Anything that strengthens your bond with your spouse and causes you two to come together in like-mindedness will be considered dangerous to Satan, and he'll do what it takes to prevent it—through distractions, misunderstandings, interruptions, feelings of intimidation, personal insecurities, fatigue, and so on. That doesn't mean every time your prayer time is interrupted or needs to be postponed that it was the work of the devil. Nor does it mean each time your spouse needs to cancel or doesn't feel like praying it is his fault. It just means that our battle "is not against flesh and blood, but against the rulers, against the authorities, against the powers of this dark world and against the spiritual forces of evil in the heavenly realms" (Ephesians 6:12).

Pushing Through the Obstacles

Just as there are many reasons why it's difficult for couples to pray together, there are equally as many ways to push through the barriers and incorporate a habit that will draw the two of you closer to one another and closer to God.

1. *Pray it through.* Talk to God first about your desire to pray with your husband. First John 5:14-15 assures us that "if we ask anything according to his will, he hears us. And if we know that he hears us—whatever we ask—we know that we have what we have asked of him." So ask God for the time in your schedule and for wisdom in how to suggest it to your spouse, and ask Him to prepare the heart of your spouse to desire this time with you as well.
2. *Set a time.* By setting an agreed-upon appointment for prayer with your spouse, both of you are more likely to keep it. But, as with any appointment, there will be times you or your husband will need to postpone or reschedule. That's life. So be flexible, and extend grace.
3. *Ease into it.* There's a reason prayer is considered a spiritual discipline. And as with any habit or discipline, it will take work. So ease into it. You might even start with praying together once a week for a brief time, then gradually increase your prayer time to two or three times a week until it becomes part of your daily schedule.
4. *Keep it short.* There is nothing wrong with limiting the time that the two of you can spend in prayer, especially when you're first starting out. There are jobs to be done, tasks to complete, and children to care for. Be respectful of each

other's time and put parameters around how long your prayer time will be. My husband often instructs couples to approach prayer as he would lead a team of backpackers. When a group of backpackers hit the trail, there's a general rule of thumb that says everyone should walk at a pace that is most doable for the slowest-moving member of the team. It's the "leave no man (or woman) behind" motto. So let the spouse who tends to pray the shortest set the tempo.

5. *Keep it simple.* You can keep it short *and* simple by limiting your prayer time together to the basic or most pressing needs on your heart. A couple's prayer time should never replace an individual's prayer time. And in my opinion, our prayer time alone with God, one-on-one, should far outweigh the amount of time we pray with our spouse. God is always there. He's always available. And you don't need to schedule a time to talk with Him. But that's often not the case with your husband. Respect his time and pray only about pressing needs that concern your family, such as job, health, or financial issues, the salvation or spiritual life of loved ones, the behavioral issues of your children, and so on. You might even consider praying together for certain things on certain days: Monday—God's provision; Tuesday—family and extended family; Wednesday—ministry opportunities; and so on.

6. *Keep it safe.* Remove any possibility of intimidation by assuring your husband that your prayer time together is not an arena for judgment or assumption. In other words, anything that is prayed for is "safe"—and won't be analyzed, critiqued, shared with others, or brought up again in a non-supportive way.

7. *Keep it light.* I don't mean to sound irreverent here or to imply our prayers should be shallow. I mean "light" in terms of encouraging. Praying with your husband about

sensitive issues in your marriage or situations in your past that may cause him to feel regret or remorse might not be best, especially if you're just starting out. Save the heavier, deeply personal issues for time with just you and God. The Lord can handle them, and many times your husband won't know what to do upon hearing prayers that might be directed at him or any trouble or anxiety he may be causing you or your marriage or family. Aim for a goal of togetherness and encouragement as you pray. If your goal is that both you and your husband emerge from that prayer time feeling more empowered and strengthened together, then you will know what to address while praying with your husband and what to keep for an extended prayer time between just you and God. As you begin praying together regularly, the Holy Spirit may impress upon your hearts to pray about deeper issues, and when that is the case, you both will simply be following His lead.

8. *Finally, you can apply the principles of Philippians 2:1-2 as a guideline in praying together by "being of the same mind, maintaining the same love, united in spirit, intent on one purpose"* (NASB). That one purpose or goal should be that each of you emerge from your prayer time together feeling stronger, more supported, and more unified in order to take on the enemy of your souls.

Encouragement and Advice from Couples

I asked several couples to share the key to their connection, the best advice they can offer another couple, or just what has worked best for them. Here is what they had to say:

As You Draw Closer to God, You'll Draw Closer to One Another

Dawn Marie shared the key to a close connection with her husband:

> "Early in our marriage we both heard an evangelist say, 'Wives, the closer you get to the Lord, and, husbands, the closer you get to the Lord, the closer you will be drawn to each other.' He described it like a triangle, and in that word picture we clearly saw how closeness to Christ encouraged closeness to our spouse. This became the foundation in our marriage that helped us make sense of both the good times and the tough times. When we were both walking closely with the Lord, we sensed that tremendous bond of marital unity. And when one or both of us struggled, we remembered why we might be drifting in our relationship. That encouraged us to scurry back into fellowship with Christ, which in turn enabled closer fellowship with each other. It's all been about that 'triangle' relationship. In the early

days of marriage, my wedding ring—with a triangle formation of diamonds—was a constant illustration of that important truth."

Aim to Serve One Another

Greg and Julie Gorman are authors of *Two Are Better Than One: God Has a Purpose for Your Marriage.* Julie said the secret to their successful marriage isn't one or two certain things she does or doesn't do. "It's just been more of a lifelong pursuit to serve one another instead of expecting to be served," she said. "When our attitude is, *How can I serve you? How can I make your life better today?* we will not be so focused on ourselves."

Stand Firmly by Him in the Crisis, Not Just the Celebrations

A friend of mine who is a pastor's wife and has a strong marriage of more than 40 years has seen the value of standing by her husband in the crisis moments, not just the celebrations.

> "We served in a church and, through a series of difficult circumstances, needed to resign. There was an opportunity when I could have blamed my husband for part of the situation; but instead, I chose to stand beside him and present a united front. We have long forgotten all the awful details in the crisis, but he has never forgotten my resolve to trust him and his leadership. God grew his character through the difficulty, but even more He strengthened our bond of trust."

Make an Effort to Be on the Same Page

Tyler said the key to his closeness with Connie, ten years after they married, is that they both work hard to be on the same page.

> "It comes down to communication. Thankfully, we've been on the same page about nearly every moral and important thing in our married life, including personal values, ministry, parenting, family decisions, and so on. But we always

> talk things through and consider each other before making decisions. We communicate and talk things through so that we are both on the same page when moving forward in the smallest things, from dinner choices (especially when one of us plans meals for two weeks at a time) to a conversation we had about starting sex/relationship/marriage conversations with our daughter."

Develop Shared Interests

Chris, who has been married to Dan for nearly 30 years, said developing shared interests throughout their married life has helped them stay connected. Now that their children are grown, they share with each other the love of grandparenting.

> "We have shared goals and passions—primarily serving and being involved in our kids' and grandkids' lives. As our adult children have grown, it has given us both great joy to be able to help them realize their dreams and come alongside them in practical ways, like helping them move, watching their children, and treating them to nights out. Dan and I are similar in our work ethic and commitment to our family. I see that as one of our greatest strengths."

Have a Marriage Mentor—or a Few

Misty, whose story we read about in chapter 11, is now experiencing her "second honeymoon" with her husband after 15 years. She advised,

> "Find marriage mentors who are willing to hold you accountable. Meet with them monthly and have transparent but thoughtful discussions on what stumbling blocks you are having with each other. Our marriage mentors and marriage class instructors taught my husband and me how to enhance our communication by asking the clarifying question of, 'How so?' when we are feeling disrespected or neglected. This tool gives both of us a safe path to unpack unrealistic expectations or misunderstandings."

Chris reinforced the idea of having a mentor:

> "I think naturally, over time, as you and your husband have a history to draw from, trust, passion, and understanding grow. I recommend seeking out a couple that has been lovingly and respectfully (not necessarily 'happily') married for a while to come alongside to help mentor and pray for your marriage."

And Robin Reinke said that even though she and her husband, Jeff, are marriage counselors:

> "My husband and I have through the years invested in personal counselors and mentors who have helped us keep emotionally connected and growing spiritually and relationally. We have also made a commitment to attend a marriage retreat or weekend getaway each year to pour into our marriage."

Honor Each Other in Sickness and in Health

Allison and Guy have enjoyed a very active lifestyle...mountain biking, snorkeling, skiing, you name it. Yet the past few years have presented challenges for them as they've both experienced health issues.

> "After many years of excellent health, we have each experienced big physical illnesses or accidents. As a result, we've been taking turns over the years caring for each other during times of illness. Empathizing and physically caring for one another gave us so much more understanding for each other. We had to walk the walk, and then we understood so much more. It is humbling, but powerful. Sharing our fears about cancer, or the potential changes to our ability to provide for our family, or the ability to enjoy our favorite activities bonded us together in sympathy and understanding. Yet we were able to reassure each other that even in hard times, we were committed and would stick together with God's power and as God intended, even when the

> future looked very different from the one we had planned. It sounds so cliché, but we knew God was sovereign over our lives and we trusted Him to work things for our good—even when it didn't feel good at the time. We looked for the good and yet could agree that the bad parts really stunk. That is important too!"

Pray for Your Husband

Allison said another way to get through those tough times, like accidents or illnesses, that you don't plan on going through is to constantly pray for your husband.

> "Memorize verses to pray for your husband and pray for him regularly, believing and trusting God to work in your husband's life to grow him into the man God would have him to be, just as you are growing in your relationship with Christ. Have confidence in the power of God and in prayer."

Notes

Chapter 1: Consider His Heart

1. Romans 6:2,4,11; Galatians 2:20; Colossians 3:3.

Chapter 2: Think It Through

1. *The Woman's Study Bible* (Nashville, TN: Thomas Nelson Publishers, 1995), 1104.
2. Eugene H. Peterson, *The Message: The Bible in Contemporary Language* (Colorado Springs: Navpress, 2002), 1182.
3. *The Woman's Study Bible*, 1105.
4. *The Woman's Study Bible*, 1109.
5. *The Woman's Study Bible*, 1113.
6. *The Woman's Study Bible*, 1118.
7. *The Woman's Study Bible*, 1120.

Chapter 3: Keep Him First

1. *The Woman's Study Bible*, 47.

Chapter 4: Let It Go

1. For more on this, see my book *When a Woman Overcomes Life's Hurts: Discover the Healing and Wholeness God Has for You*, which is available for order on my website: www.StrengthForTheSoul.com.

Chapter 5: Switch It Up

1. For more on this concept, see our book *When Couples Walk Together: 31 Days to a Closer Connection* (Eugene, OR: Harvest House Publishers, 2010).

Chapter 8: Close the Gap

1. This can be found in the online article located at https://stearns-law.com/resources/blog/divorce/the-top-10-reasons-marriages-end-in-divorce.

Chapter 9: Help Him Out

1. Dr. Gary and Barbara Rosberg, *6 Secrets to a Lasting Love* (Carol Stream, IL: Tyndale House, 2006), 187.
2. This paragraph is taken from my book *When a Woman Inspires Her Husband* (Eugene, OR: Harvest House Publishers, 2011), 36.

Chapter 11: Stick It Out

1. Cindi and Hugh McMenamin, *When Couples Walk Together: 31 Days to a Closer Connection* (Eugene, OR: Harvest House Publishers, 2010), 190.

Chapter 12: Bring It Back

1. J. Parker is the author of *Hot, Holy, and Humorous: Sex in Marriage by God's Design* and blogs at Hot, Holy & Humorous, using a biblical perspective and a blunt sense of humor to foster godly sexuality. She has been married for 23 years and holds a master's degree in counseling. This article was published at Crosswalk.com, November 7, 2016.
2. Greg and Julie Gorman, *Two Are Better Than One: God Has a Purpose for Your Marriage* (Racine, WI: BroadStreet Publishing, 2016), 87.

Dying to Self in Your Marriage

1. For more on developing and maintaining an intimate relationship with God, see my book *Letting God Meet Your Emotional Needs* by Harvest House Publishers.

An Invitation to Write

How have you grown closer to God and your husband through this book? I would love to hear from you and encourage you personally, and pray for you and your husband as well.

You can find me online at www.StrengthForTheSoul.com. Leave me a message that you were there and let me know how I can pray for you. I try my best to respond to all my readers.

You can connect with me on Facebook too at Strength for the Soul.

Or you can send me a letter at:

Cindi McMenamin
c/o Harvest House Publishers
990 Owen Loop North
Eugene, OR 97402

To contact me to speak to your group, or to find out how you can have my husband and me bring a "Couples' Date Night" to your church, e-mail me at:

Cindi@StrengthForTheSoul.com

Books by Cindi McMenamin

10 Secrets to Becoming a Worry-Free Mom

Drama Free

God's Whispers to a Woman's Heart

Letting God Meet Your Emotional Needs

When a Mom Inspires Her Daughter

When a Woman Discovers Her Dream

When a Woman Inspires Her Husband

When a Woman Overcomes Life's Hurts

When Couples Walk Together

When God Pursues a Woman's Heart

When God Sees Your Tears

When Women Long for Rest

When Women Walk Alone

When You're Running on Empty

Women on the Edge

You know what drama is...in your circle of friends, in your workplace, in your extended family, and in the unexpected circumstances of life. But has it gotten to be too much?

Truth is, we've all been both actor and audience when it comes to life's dramas. But you don't have to let them sweep you away.

Discover a biblical script for a more peaceful life as you learn how to...

- dial down the drama in your own life
- respond appropriately to situations that would otherwise escalate
- view high-maintenance individuals through the eyes of Christ

The world may be a stage—but you can find freedom from the drama.

Women long to be loved, to be known, to be understood. But who can meet those needs at their deepest level? Only the One who created women—who knows them by name and who designed them—can bring fulfillment that truly satisfies.

Letting God Meet Your Emotional Needs shows how God desires to help every woman:

- I need acceptance...God loves, forgives, and accepts.
- I need security...God promises He will never leave.
- I need communication...God talks to me intimately through His Word.

The demands of everyday life almost always pull husbands and wives in different directions. And even when they are together, there's very little opportunity to just be a couple. Work, children, and other commitments make it a constant challenge to find quality time alone.

Each reading in this 31-day book offers simple, helpful (and fun!) steps a husband and wife can take to nourish closeness and intimacy. Among the topics are

- the power of a note
- making a memory
- extending grace
- splurging on love
- finding a getaway

Key thoughts from Scripture are interwoven into each devotion, and each ends with an application section called "Going the Extra Mile" as well as a couple's prayer. Especially helpful are the frequent anecdotal tips from a woman's perspective (Cindi) and a man's (Hugh).